The Kama Sutra

The Kama Sutra

Translated by
Sir Richard F. Burton

Edited and with an introduction by
John Baldock

Indigo
PRESS

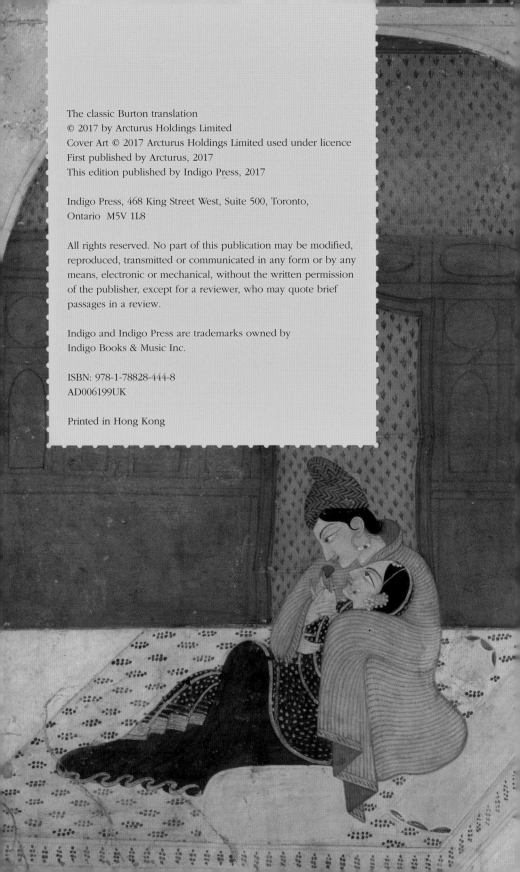

ISBN: 978-1-78828-444-8
AD006199UK

Printed in Hong Kong

CONTENTS

INTRODUCTION

THE REPUTATION THE *KAMA SUTRA* (*Aphorisms on Love*) has gained as a manual for the sexually adventurous is such that the two words 'kama sutra' have now become a synonym for sex and a convenient brand name for the promotion of all things sexual. Yet prior to the 1960s this 3rd-century Sanskrit text had been virtually unknown in the English-speaking world because its circulation was limited to a few privately published, under-the-counter editions. In fact, the book might have remained unknown in the West but for its chance rediscovery in the late 19th century by Sir Richard Burton (1821–1890), the British diplomat, explorer and orientalist.

Burton was working with two Indian Sanskrit scholars on an English translation of a 16th-century sex manual, the *Ananga Ranga* (*The Stage of Love*), when his curiosity was aroused by the text's frequent references to a certain sage by the name of Vatsyayana. On learning that Vatsyayana was the author of the *Kama Sutra*, the classic Sanskrit text on love, Burton asked his co-translators to obtain a copy. But as complete copies of Vatsyayana's text were by then difficult to find, the two scholars recompiled it by comparing four different copies borrowed from Sanskrit libraries. The text was then translated into English and published privately in Benares in 1883 by the Kama Shastra Society, which had been founded by Burton and Forster Fitzgerald Arbuthnot, a British colonial official and translator, as a means of bypassing the obscenity laws of the time. The breakthrough that permitted the open publication of the *Kama Sutra* and other works previously classified as obscene occurred in the 1960s in the wake of the 1959 Obscene Publications Act and the landmark trial of 1961 in which Penguin, the publisher of D H Lawrence's *Lady Chatterley's Lover*, won approval for the book's publication on the grounds of its literary merit. Shortly afterwards Burton's translation of the *Kama Sutra* was published openly in both the UK and USA, an event that coincided with the dawning of the sexual revolution of the 1960s. However, contrary to the reputation it has since gained as a sex manual, the *Kama Sutra* is primarily a guide to choosing an appropriate partner; how to conduct oneself during courtship, betrothal and marriage; acceptable social pastimes; the ideal siting of a house and the arrangement of its rooms and furniture – only one section of the book is devoted to explicit sexual activity.

Although the Sanskrit word *Kama* is widely translated as love or sexual desire, it actually refers to aesthetic or sensual pleasure in general. As such it is one of the four goals of life (the *purusharthas*) of Hinduism – the three others are *Dharma* (religious duty or right conduct), *Artha* (worldly status) and *Moksha* (spiritual liberation). The rules governing the pursuit of these goals are a central theme of the vast corpus of Sanskrit texts or scriptures, the original authorship of which is traditionally attributed to the 'Lord of Beings' who, at the same time as he created men and women, laid down the rules for human existence in 'one hundred thousand chapters'. As Vatsyayana explains in the *Kama Sutra*, the rules governing Dharma were transcribed by Manu (the first man and the first king to rule this earth); the rules governing Artha were compiled by Brihaspati (a Hindu deity); and those governing Kama were 'expounded by Nandi, the follower of Mahadeva [i.e. the Hindu god Shiva]'.

One of the world's oldest religions, Hinduism evolved over many centuries in the course of which its three principal deities – Vishnu, Shiva and The Goddess or Divine Mother – were represented in a variety of forms and guises and acquired additional names. In Hinduism as in many other ancient religious traditions, the relationship between humans and the cosmos was maintained by the gods, personifications of the invisible forces governing the universe. Likewise, the primordial creative act that brought the universe into being and continues to sustain it was envisaged as the union of male and female creative energies and was thus frequently personified in the lovemaking of a male deity and his consort. According to an ancient tradition, Nandi (the white bull, Shiva's gatekeeper) overheard Shiva making love with his consort Parvati and it was this that moved him to utter the sacred text of the *Kama Sutra*, thus making the sensual pleasures enjoyed by the gods available to us mere mortals.

Little is known about the life of Vatsyayana, but various authorities suggest that he lived in the third century. He was clearly a devout man, for at the end of his book he describes how it 'was composed, according to the precepts of Holy Writ, for the benefit of the world, by Vatsyayana, while leading the life of a religious student, and wholly engaged in the contemplation of the Deity.' Elsewhere he explains that the *Kama Sutra* originally comprised 1,000 chapters, which were subsequently abbreviated by a succession of authors before being divided into seven parts, each of which was rewritten by further authors. As a result of this division the original text lost its cohesion and so, to render it accessible to its intended audience, Vatsyayana distilled the work of his predecessors and composed a single, small volume that is the *Kama Sutra* as we know it today. But the sources of sensual pleasure extend beyond those contained in the *Kama Sutra*, which was the earliest text in a genre that became known as the *Kama Shastra* (*The Rules or Science of Pleasure*). Vatsyayana lists a further sixty-four practices or arts, ranging from singing and dancing to composing poems, that form part of the *Kama Shastra* and which should be studied alongside the *Kama Sutra*. However, he also reminds us that *Kama* is not the only goal to be pursued in this life. It is the practice of *Dharma*, *Artha* and *Kama* together that has the potential to lead to true happiness.

ABOUT THIS EDITION

For many centuries the *Kama Sutra* appeared in text-only form and it was not until the 15th century that the various sexual positions began to be illustrated in miniature paintings. Many of the illustrations accompanying the present text were produced in the studios of the Rajput states of Rajasthan, north-western India. These studios flourished from the early 17th century onwards and while some were strongly influenced by Mughal art following the Mughal conquest of Rajasthan in the 16th century, others remained comparatively free of such influence, hence the wide variations of style. In some paintings the artist has used shading to give form to naturalistic figures and rudimentary perspective to create a sense of space. In others the artist has employed a much more decorative, less realistic style in which the emphasis is on the patterns created by the flattened shapes of the different elements of the composition. Although the widespread depiction of the sexual positions described in the *Kama Sutra* was a relatively recent development in painting, the same is not true of sculpture – from the 5th century onwards couples embracing in a variety of positions had featured among the profusion of carvings that decorated Hindu temples.

Burton's translation of Vatsyayana's text is presented in the following pages in an abridged form. In keeping with a practice common among Sanskrit authors, Vatsyayana's original text included several lengthy passages in which he debated the pros and cons of certain propositions, either his own or those put forward by earlier authors. These have been omitted from this abridged edition, as have a number of lists that were of specific relevance to the period when the *Kama Sutra* was written and which included variations in the customs and practices of different regions of India. Also omitted are four chapters from Part Six which contained advice for the courtesan on getting rid of unwanted lovers as well as the socioeconomic gains and losses that were concomitant with her profession. Part Seven of Vatsyayana's text, which comprised two chapters containing archaic recipes for tonics and stimulants, has likewise been omitted.

The final words of this introduction are best left to Vatsyayana:

'This work is not intended to be used merely as an instrument for satisfying our desires. A person, acquainted with the true principles of this science, and who preserves his Dharma, Artha, *and* Kama, *and has regard for the practices of the people, is sure to obtain the mastery over his senses.*

'In short, an intelligent and prudent person, attending to Dharma *and* Artha, *and attending to* Kama *also, without becoming the slave of his passions, obtains success in everything that he may undertake.'*

John Baldock

PART ONE

INTRODUCTORY

CHAPTER 1

PREFACE

IN THE BEGINNING, THE LORD of Beings created men and women, and in the form of commandments in one hundred thousand chapters laid down rules for regulating their existence with regard to *Dharma*[1], *Artha*[2], and *Kama*[3]. Some of these commandments, namely those which treated of *Dharma*, were separately written by Swayambhu Manu; those that related to *Artha* were compiled by Brihaspati; and those that referred to *Kama* were expounded by Nandi, the follower of Mahadeva, in one thousand chapters.

Now these *Kama Sutra* (*Aphorisms on Love*), written by Nandi in one thousand chapters, were reproduced by Shvetaketu, the son of Uddvalaka, in an abbreviated form in five hundred chapters, and this work was again similarly reproduced in an abridged form, in one hundred and fifty chapters, by Babhravya, an inheritant of the Punchala (South of Delhi) country. These one hundred and fifty chapters were then put together under seven heads or parts named severally:

1. *Sadharana* (general topics)
2. *Samprayogika* (embraces, etc.)
3. *Kanya Samprayuktaka* (union of males and females)
4. *Bharyadhikarika* (on one's own wife)
5. *Paradika* (on the wives of other people)
6. *Vaisika* (on courtesans)
7. *Aupamishadika* (on the arts of seduction, tonic medicines, etc.)[4]

The sixth part of this last work was separately expounded by Dattaka at the request of the public women of Pataliputra (Patna), and in the same way Charayana explained the first part of it. The remaining parts, viz. the second, third, fourth, fifth, and seventh, were each separately expounded by

- Suvarnanabha (second part)
- Ghotakamukha (third part)
- Gonardiya (fourth part)

Gonikaputra (fifth part)

 Kuchumara (seventh part), respectively.

Thus the work being written in parts by different authors was almost unobtainable and, as the parts which were expounded by Dattaka and the others treated only of the particular branches of the subject to which each part related, and moreover as the original work of Babhravya was difficult to be mastered on account of its length, Vatsyayana, therefore, composed his work in a small volume as an abstract of the whole of the works of the above-named authors.

1 *Dharma* is acquisition of religious merit.

2 *Artha* is acquisition of wealth and property, etc.

3 *Kama* is love, pleasure and sensual gratification. These three words are retained throughout in their original, as technical terms. They may also be defined as virtue, wealth and pleasure.

4 Editor's note: Part Seven has been omitted from this edition.

CHAPTER 2

ON THE ACQUISITION OF
DHARMA, _ARTHA_ AND _KAMA_

MAN, THE PERIOD OF WHOSE LIFE is one hundred years,
should practise _Dharma_, _Artha_ and _Kama_ at different times and in such
a manner that they may harmonize together and not clash in any way.
He should acquire learning in his childhood, in his youth and middle
age he should attend to _Artha_ and _Kama_, and in his old age he should
perform _Dharma_, and thus seek to gain _Moksha_, i.e. release from further
transmigration. Or, on account of the uncertainty of life, he may
practise them at times when they are enjoined to be practised. But one
thing is to be noted, he should lead the life of a religious student until
he finishes his education.

Dharma is obedience to the command of the _Shastra_, or Holy Writ,
of the Hindus to do certain things, such as the performance of sacrifices,
which are not generally done, because they do not belong to this world, and
produce no visible effect; and not to do other things, such as eating meat,
which is often done because it belongs to this world, and has visible effects.

Dharma should be learnt from the _Shruti_ (Holy Writ), and from those
conversant with it.

Artha is the acquisition of arts, land, gold, cattle, wealth, equipages and
friends. It is, further, the protection of what is acquired, and the increase of
what is protected.

Artha should be learnt from the king's officers, and from merchants who
may be versed in the ways of commerce.

Kama is the enjoyment of appropriate objects by the five senses of
hearing, feeling, seeing, tasting and smelling, assisted by the mind together
with the soul. The ingredient in this is a peculiar contact between the
organ of sense and its object, and the consciousness of pleasure which
arises from that contact is called _Kama_.

Kama is to be learnt from the _Kama Sutra_ (_Aphorisms on Love_) and from
the practice of citizens.

When all the three, viz. *Dharma*, *Artha* and *Kama*, come together, the former is better than the one which follows it, i.e. *Dharma* is better than *Artha*, and *Artha* is better than *Kama*. But *Artha* should always be first practised by the king for the livelihood of men is to be obtained from it only. Again, *Kama* being the occupation of public women, they should prefer it to the other two, and these are exceptions to the general rule.

Thus a man practising *Dharma*, *Artha* and *Kama* enjoys happiness both in this world and in the world to come. The good perform those actions in which there is no fear as to what is to result from them in the next world, and in which there is no danger to their welfare. Any action which conduces to the practice of *Dharma*, *Artha* and *Kama* together, or of any two, or even one of them, should be performed, but an action which conduces to the practice of one of them at the expense of the remaining two should not be performed.

CHAPTER 3

ON THE ARTS AND SCIENCES TO BE STUDIED

MAN SHOULD STUDY THE *KAMA SUTRA* and the arts and sciences subordinate thereto, in addition to the study of the arts and sciences contained in *Dharma* and *Artha*. Even young maids should study this *Kama Sutra* along with its arts and sciences before marriage, and after it they should continue to do so with the consent of their husbands.

Here some learned men object, and say that females, not being allowed to study any science, should not study the *Kama Sutra*.

But Vatsyayana is of opinion that this objection does not hold good, for women already know the practice of *Kama Sutra*, and that practice is derived from the *Kama Shastra*, or the science of *Kama* itself. Moreover, it is not only in this but in many other cases that, though the practice of a science is known to all, only a few persons are acquainted with the rules and laws on which the science is based. Thus the *Yadnikas* or sacrificers, though ignorant of grammar, make use of appropriate words when addressing the different Deities, and do not know how these words are framed. Again, persons do the duties required of them on auspicious days, which are fixed by astrology, though they are not acquainted with the science of astrology. In a like manner riders of horses and elephants train these animals without knowing the science of training animals, but from practice only. And similarly the people of the most distant provinces obey the laws of the kingdom from practice, and because there is a king over them, and without further reason.[1] And from experience we find that some women, such as daughters of princes and their ministers, and public women, are actually versed in the *Kama Shastra*.

A female, therefore, should learn the *Kama Shastra*, or at least a part of it, by studying its practice from some confidential friend. She should study alone in private the sixty-four practices that form a part of the

Kama Shastra. Her teacher should be one of the following persons: the daughter of a nurse brought up with her and already married,[2] or a female friend who can be trusted in everything, or the sister of her mother (i.e. her aunt), or an old female servant, or a female beggar who may have formerly lived in the family, or her own sister who can always be trusted.

The following are the arts to be studied, together with the *Kama Sutra*:

- Singing
- Playing on musical instruments
- Dancing
- Union of dancing, singing, and playing instrumental music
- Writing and drawing
- Tattooing
- Arraying and adorning an idol with rice and flowers
- Spreading and arranging beds or couches of flowers, or flowers upon the ground
- Colouring the teeth, garments, hair, nails and bodies, i.e. staining, dyeing, colouring and painting the same
- Fixing stained glass into a floor
- The art of making beds, and spreading out carpets and cushions for reclining
- Playing on musical glasses filled with water
- Storing and accumulating water in aqueducts, cisterns and reservoirs
- Picture making, trimming and decorating
- Stringing of rosaries, necklaces, garlands and wreaths
- Binding of turbans and chaplets, and making crests and top-knots of flowers
- Scenic representations, stage playing
- Art of making ear ornaments
- Art of preparing perfumes and odours
- Proper disposition of jewels and decorations, and adornment in dress
- Magic or sorcery
- Quickness of hand or manual skill
- Culinary art, i.e. cooking and cookery
- Making lemonades, sherbets, acidulated drinks, and spirituous extracts with proper flavour and colour
- Tailor's work and sewing
- Making parrots, flowers, tufts, tassels, bunches, bosses, knobs, etc., out of yarn or thread
- Solution of riddles, enigmas, covert speeches, verbal puzzles and enigmatical questions
- A game, which consisted in repeating verses, and as one person finished, another person had to commence at once, repeating another verse, beginning with the same letter with which the last

speaker's verse ended, whoever failed to repeat was considered to have lost, and to be subject to pay a forfeit or stake of some kind

- The art of mimicry or imitation
- Reading, including chanting and intoning
- Study of sentences difficult to pronounce. It is played as a game chiefly by women and children and consists of a difficult sentence being given, and when repeated quickly, the words are often transposed or badly pronounced
- Practice with sword, single stick, quarter staff and bow and arrow
- Drawing inferences, reasoning or inferring
- Carpentry, or the work of a carpenter
- Architecture, or the art of building
- Knowledge about gold and silver coins, and jewels and gems
- Chemistry and mineralogy
- Colouring jewels, gems and beads
- Knowledge of mines and quarries
- Gardening; knowledge of treating the diseases of trees and plants, of nourishing them, and determining their ages
- Art of cock fighting, quail fighting and ram fighting
- Art of teaching parrots and starlings to speak
- Art of applying perfumed ointments to the body, and of dressing the hair with unguents and perfumes and braiding it
- The art of understanding writing in cypher, and the writing of words in a peculiar way
- The art of speaking by changing the forms of words. It is of various kinds. Some speak by changing the beginning and end of words, others by adding unnecessary letters between every syllable of a word, and so on
- Knowledge of language and of the vernacular dialects
- Art of making flower carriages
- Art of framing mystical diagrams, of addressing spells and charms, and binding armlets
- Mental exercises, such as completing stanzas or verses on receiving a part of them; or supplying one, two or three lines when the remaining lines are given indiscriminately from different verses, so as to make the whole an entire verse with regard to its meaning; or arranging the words of a verse written irregularly by separating the vowels from the consonants, or leaving them out altogether; or putting into verse or prose sentences represented by signs or symbols. There are many other such exercises.
- Composing poems

- Knowledge of dictionaries and vocabularies
- Knowledge of ways of changing and disguising the appearance of persons
- Knowledge of the art of changing the appearance of things, such as making cotton to appear as silk, coarse and common things to appear as fine and good
- Various ways of gambling
- Art of obtaining possession of the property of others by means of mantras or incantations
- Skill in youthful sports
- Knowledge of the rules of society, and of how to pay respect and compliments to others
- Knowledge of the art of war, of arms, of armies, etc.
- Knowledge of gymnastics
- Art of knowing the character of a man from his features
- Knowledge of scanning or constructing verses
- Arithmetical recreations
- Making artificial flowers
- Making figures and images in clay.

A public woman, endowed with a good disposition, beauty and other winning qualities, and also versed in the above arts, obtains the name of a *Ganika*, or public woman of high quality, and receives a seat of honour in an assemblage of men. She is, moreover, always respected by the king, and praised by learned men, and her favour being sought for by all, she becomes an object of universal regard. The daughter of a king too as well as the daughter of a minister, being learned in the above arts, can make their husbands favourable to them. And in the same manner, if a wife becomes separated from her husband, and falls into distress, she can support herself easily, even in a foreign country, by means of her knowledge of these arts. Even the bare knowledge of them gives attractiveness to a woman. A man who is versed in these arts, who is loquacious and acquainted with the arts of gallantry, gains very soon the hearts of women, even though he is only acquainted with them for a short time.

---

1 The author wishes to prove that a great many things are done by people from practice and custom, without their being acquainted with the reason of things, or the laws on which they are based, and this is perfectly true.

2 The proviso of being married applies to all the teachers.

CHAPTER 4

THE LIFE OF A CITIZEN

HAVING THUS ACQUIRED LEARNING, a man, with the wealth that he may have gained by gift, conquest, purchase, deposit,[1] or inheritance from his ancestors, should become a householder,[2] and pass the life of a citizen.[3] He should take a house in a city, or large village, or in the vicinity of good men, or in a place which is the resort of many persons. This abode should be situated near some water, and divided into different compartments for different purposes. It should be surrounded by a garden, and also contain two rooms, an outer and an inner one. The inner room should be occupied by the females, while the outer room, balmy with rich perfumes, should contain a bed, soft, agreeable to the sight, covered with a clean white cloth, low in the middle part, having garlands and bunches of flowers[4] upon it, and a canopy above it, and two pillows, one at the top, another at the bottom. There should be also a sort of couch besides, and at the head of this a sort of stool, on which should be placed the fragrant ointments for the night, as well as flowers. Near the couch, on the ground, there should be a box containing ornaments, a board for drawing, a pot containing perfume, some books, and some garlands of the yellow amaranth flowers; outside the outer room there should be cages of birds, and a separate place for spinning, carving and such like diversions. In the garden there should be a whirling swing and a common swing, as also a bower of creepers covered with flowers, in which a raised parterre should be made for sitting.

Now the householder, having got up in the morning and performed his necessary duties,[5] should wash his teeth, apply a limited quantity of ointments and perfumes to his body, put some ornaments on his person and collyrium on his eyelids and below his eyes, colour his lips with alacktaka,[6] and look at himself in the glass. Having then eaten betel leaves, with other things that give fragrance to the mouth, he should

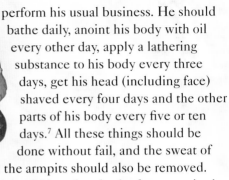

perform his usual business. He should bathe daily, anoint his body with oil every other day, apply a lathering substance to his body every three days, get his head (including face) shaved every four days and the other parts of his body every five or ten days.[7] All these things should be done without fail, and the sweat of the armpits should also be removed.

Meals should be taken in the forenoon, in the afternoon, and again at night. After breakfast, parrots and other birds should be taught to speak, and the fighting of cocks, quails, and rams should follow. A limited time should be devoted to diversions with *Pithamardas*, *Vitas*, and *Vidushakas*,[8] and then should be taken the midday sleep.[9] After this the householder, having put on his clothes and ornaments, should, during the afternoon, converse with his friends. In the evening there should be singing, and after that the householder, along with his friend, should await in his room, previously decorated and perfumed, the arrival of the woman that may be attached to him, or he may send a female messenger for her, or go for her himself. After her arrival at his house, he and his friend should welcome her, and entertain her with a loving and agreeable conversation. Thus end the duties of the day.

The following are the things to be done occasionally as diversions or amusements:

- Holding festivals[10] in honour of different Deities
- Social gatherings of both sexes
- Drinking parties
- Picnics
- Other social diversions.

FESTIVALS

On some particular auspicious day, an assembly of citizens should be convened in the temple of Saraswati.[11] There the skill of singers, and of others who may have come recently to the town, should be tested, and on the following day they should always be given some rewards.

After that they may either be retained or dismissed, according as their performances are liked or not by the assembly. The members of the assembly should act in concert, both in times of distress as well as in times of prosperity, and it is also the duty of these citizens to show hospitality to strangers who may have come to the assembly. What is said above should be understood to apply to all the other festivals which may be held in honour of the different Deities, according to the present rules.

SOCIAL GATHERINGS

When men of the same age, disposition and talents, fond of the same diversions and with the same degree of education, sit together in company with public women,[12] or in an assembly of citizens, or at the abode of one among themselves, and engage in agreeable discourse with each other, such is called a 'sitting in company' or a social gathering. The subjects of discourse are to be the completion of verses half-composed by others, and the testing the knowledge of one another in the various arts. The women who may be the most beautiful, who may like the same things that the men like, and who may have power to attract the minds of others, are here done homage to.

DRINKING PARTIES

Men and women should drink in one another's houses. And here the men should cause the public women to drink, and should then drink themselves, liquors such as the Madhu, Aireya, Sara and Asawa, which are of bitter and sour taste; also drinks concocted from the barks of various trees, wild fruits and leaves.

GOING TO GARDENS OR PICNICS

In the forenoon, men having dressed themselves should go to gardens on horseback, accompanied by public women and followed by servants. And having done there all the duties of the day, and passed the time in various agreeable diversions, they should return home in

the afternoon in the same manner, bringing with them bunches of flowers, etc.

The same also applies to bathing in summer in water from which wicked or dangerous animals have previously been taken out, and which has been built in on all sides.

OTHER SOCIAL DIVERSIONS

Spending nights playing with dice. Going out on moonlight nights. Keeping the festive day in honour of spring. Plucking the sprouts and fruits of the mango trees. Eating the fibres of lotuses. Eating the tender ears of corn. Picnicking in the forests when the trees get their new foliage. The *Udakakashvedika* or sporting in the water. Decorating each other with the flowers of some trees. Pelting each other with the flowers of the Kadamba tree, and many other sports. These and similar other amusements should always be carried on by citizens.

The above amusements should be followed by a person who diverts himself alone in company with a courtesan, as well as by a courtesan who can do the same in company with her maid servants or with citizens.

A *Pithamarda*[13] is a man without wealth, alone in the world, whose only property consists of his *Mallika*,[14] some lathering substance and a red cloth, who comes from a good country, and who is skilled in all the arts; and by teaching these arts is received in the company of citizens, and in the abode of public women.

A *Vita*[15] is a man who has enjoyed the pleasures of fortune, who is a compatriot of the citizens with whom he associates, who is possessed of the qualities of a householder, who has his wife with him, and who is honoured in the assembly of citizens and in the abodes of public women, and lives on their means and on them. A *Vidushaka*[16] (also called a *Vaihasaka*, i.e. one who provokes laughter) is a person only acquainted with some of the arts, who is a jester, and who is trusted by all.

Thus a citizen living in his town or village, respected by all, should call on the persons of his own caste who may be worth knowing. He should converse in company and gratify his friends by his society, and obliging others by his assistance in various matters, he should cause them to assist one another in the same way.

There are some verses on this subject as follows:

'*A citizen discoursing on various topics in society, obtains great respect. The wise should not resort to a society disliked by the public, governed by no rules, and intent on the destruction of others. But a learned man living in a society which acts according to the wishes of the people, and which has pleasure for its only object is highly respected in this world.'*

1 The four classes of men are the *Brahmans* or priestly class, the *Kshatriya* or warlike class, the *Vaishya* or agricultural and mercantile class, and the *Shudra* or menial class. Gift is peculiar to a *Brahman*, conquest to a

Kshatriya, while purchase, deposit, and other means of acquiring wealth belong to the *Vaishya*.

2 The four stages of life are the life of a religious student, the life of a householder, the life of a hermit, and the life of a *Sunyasi* or wandering ascetic.

3 This term would appear to apply generally to an inhabitant of Hindustan. It is not meant only for a dweller in a city.

4 Natural garden flowers.

5 The calls of nature are always performed the first thing in the morning.

6 A colour made from lac.

7 Ten days are allowed when the hair is taken out with a pair of pincers.

8 These are characters generally introduced in the Hindu drama; their characteristics will be explained further on.

9 Noonday sleep is only allowed in summer, when the nights are short.

10 These are very common in all parts of India.

11 This goddess is adored as the patroness of the fine arts, especially of music and rhetoric, as the inventress of the Sanskrit language, etc. etc. She is the goddess of harmony, eloquence and language.

12 It may be fairly considered that the courtesan (Vesya) was one of the elements, and an important element too, of early Hindu society, and that her education and intellect were both superior to that of the women of the household.

13 According to this description a *Pithamarda* would be a sort of professor of all the arts, and as such received as the friend and confidant of the citizens.

14 A seat in the form of the letter T.

15 The *Vita* is supposed to represent somewhat the character of the Parasite of the Greek comedy. It is possible that he was retained about the person of the wealthy and dissipated as a kind of private instructor, as well as an entertaining companion.

16 *Vidushaka* is evidently the buffoon and jester, and the humble companion, not the servant, of a prince or man of rank, and it is a curious peculiarity that he is always a *Brahman*.

About the Kinds of Women Resorted to by the Citizen, and of Friends and Messengers

WHEN *KAMA* IS PRACTISED BY MEN of the four castes according to the rules of the Holy Writ (i.e. by lawful marriage) with virgins of their own caste, it then becomes a means of acquiring lawful progeny and good fame, and it is not also opposed to the customs of the world. On the contrary the practice of *Kama* with women of the higher castes, and with those previously enjoyed by others, even though they be of the same caste, is prohibited. But the practice of *Kama* with women of the lower castes, with women excommunicated from their own caste, with public women, and with women twice married,[1] is neither enjoined nor prohibited. The object of practising *Kama* with such women is pleasure only.

Nayikas,[2] therefore, are of three kinds, viz. maids, women twice married, and public women. Gonikaputra has expressed an opinion that there is a fourth kind of *Nayika*, viz. a woman who is resorted to on some special occasion even though she be previously married to another. These special occasions are when a man thinks thus:

- This woman is self-willed, and has been previously enjoyed by many others besides myself. I may, therefore, safely resort to her as to a public woman though she belongs to a higher caste than mine, and, in so doing, I shall not be violating the ordinances of *Dharma*.

Or thus:

- This is a twice-married woman and has been enjoyed by others before me; there is, therefore, no objection to my resorting to her.

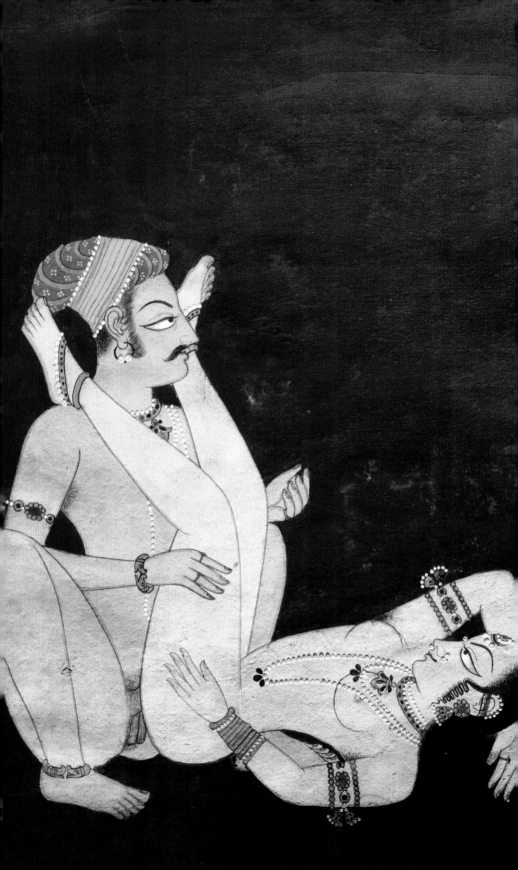

Or thus:

- This woman will turn the mind of her husband, who is very powerful, in my favour, he being at present disaffected towards me, and intent on doing me some harm.

Or thus:

- The woman whom I love is under the control of this woman. I shall, through the influence of the latter, be able to get at the former.

Or lastly thus:

- My enemy is a friend of this woman's husband, I shall therefore cause her to join him, and will thus create an enmity between her husband and him.

For these and similar other reasons the wives of other men may be resorted to, but it must be distinctly understood that is only allowed for special reasons, and not for mere carnal desire.

The following women are not to be enjoyed:

- A woman who publicly expresses desire for sexual intercourse
- A woman who is a near relation
- A woman who is a female friend
- A woman who leads the life of an ascetic
- And, lastly the wife of a relation, of a friend, of a learned *Brahman*, and of the king.

The following are of the kind of friends:

- One who has played with you in the dust, i.e. in childhood
- One who is bound by an obligation
- One who is of the same disposition and fond of the same things
- One who is a fellow student
- One who is brought up with you
- One who is an hereditary friend.

These friends should possess the following qualities:

- They should tell the truth
- They should not be changed by time
- They should be favourable to your designs
- They should be free from covetousness
- They should not be capable of being gained over by others
- They should not reveal your secrets.

A messenger should possess the following qualities:

- Skilfulness
- Boldness
- Knowledge of the intention of men by their outward signs
- Knowledge of the exact meaning of what others do or say

🙐 Good manners
🙐 Quick comprehension.

And this part ends with a verse:

'The man who is ingenious and wise, who is accompanied by a friend, and who knows the intentions of others, as also the proper time and place for doing everything, can gain over, very easily, even a woman who is very hard to be obtained.'

1 This term does not apply to a widow, but to a woman who has probably left her husband, and is living with some other person as a married woman, *maritalement*, as they say in France.

2 Any woman fit to be enjoyed without sin. The object of the enjoyment of women is twofold, *viz.* pleasure and progeny. Any woman who can be enjoyed without sin for the purpose of accomplishing either the one or the other of these two objects is a *Nayika*. The fourth kind of *Nayika* which Vatsya admits further on is neither enjoyed for pleasure or for progeny, but merely for accomplishing some special purpose in hand.

PART TWO

ON SEXUAL
UNION

KINDS OF SEXUAL UNION ACCORDING TO DIMENSIONS, FORCE OF DESIRE OR PASSION, AND TIME; AND THE DIFFERENT KINDS OF LOVE

KINDS OF UNION

MAN IS DIVIDED INTO THREE CLASSES, viz. the hare man, the bull man, and the horse man, according to the size of his *lingam*.

Woman also, according to the depth of her *yoni*, is either a female deer, a mare, or a female elephant.

There are thus three equal unions between persons of corresponding dimensions, and there are six unequal unions, when the dimensions do not correspond, or nine in all, as the following table shows:

EQUAL		UNEQUAL	
MEN	WOMEN	MEN	WOMEN
Hare	*Deer*	*Hare*	*Mare*
Bull	*Mare*	*Hare*	*Elephant*
Horse	*Elephant*	*Bull*	*Deer*
		Bull	*Elephant*
		Horse	*Deer*
		Horse	*Mare*

In these unequal unions, when the male exceeds the female in point of size, his union with a woman who is immediately next to him in size is called high union, and is of two kinds; while his union with the woman most remote from his size is called the highest union, and is of one kind only. On the other hand, when the female exceeds the male in point of size, her union with a man immediately next to her in size is called low union, and is of two kinds; while her union with a man most remote from her in size is called the lowest union, and is of one kind only.

In other words, the horse and mare, the bull and deer, form the high union, while the horse and deer form the highest union. On the female side, the elephant and bull, the mare and hare, form low unions, while the elephant and the hare make the lowest unions. There are, then, nine kinds of union according to dimensions. Amongst all these, equal unions are the best, those of a superlative degree, i.e. the highest and the lowest, are the worst, and the rest are middling, and with them the high[1] are better than the low.

There are also nine kinds of union according to the force of passion or carnal desire,
as follows:

MEN	WOMEN	MEN	WOMEN
Small	*Small*	*Small*	*Middling*
Middling	*Middling*	*Small*	*Intense*
Intense	*Intense*	*Middling*	*Small*
		Middling	*Intense*
		Intense	*Small*
		Intense	*Middling*

A man is called a man of small passion whose desire at the time of sexual union is not great, whose semen is scanty, and who cannot bear the warm embraces of the female.

Those who differ from this temperament are called men of middling passion, while those of intense passion are full of desire.

In the same way, women are supposed to have the three degrees of feeling as specified above.

Lastly, according to time there are three kinds of men and women, the short-timed, the moderate-timed, and the long-timed; and of these, as in the previous statements, there are nine kinds of union.

There being thus nine kinds of union with regard to dimensions, force of passion, and time, respectively, by making combinations of them,

innumerable kinds of union would be produced. Therefore in each particular kind of sexual union, men should use such means as they may think suitable for the occasion.[2]

At the first time of sexual union the passion of the male is intense, and his time is short, but in subsequent unions on the same day the reverse of this is the case. With the female, however, it is the contrary, for at the first time her passion is weak, and then her time long, but on subsequent occasions on the same day, her passion is intense and her time short, until her passion is satisfied.

ON THE DIFFERENT KINDS OF LOVE

Men learned in the humanities are of opinion that love is of four kinds:
- Love acquired by continual habit
- Love resulting from the imagination
- Love resulting from belief
- Love resulting from the perception of external objects.

Love resulting from the constant and continual performance of some act is called love acquired by constant practice and habit, as for instance the love of sexual intercourse, the love of hunting, the love of drinking, the love of gambling, etc., etc.

Love which is felt for things to which we are not habituated, and which proceeds entirely from ideas, is called love resulting from imagination, as for instance that love which some men and women and eunuchs feel for the *Auparishtaka* or mouth congress, and that which is felt by all for such things as embracing, kissing, etc., etc.

The love which is mutual on both sides, and proved to be true, when each looks upon the other as his or her very own, such is called love resulting from belief by the learned.

The love resulting from the perception of external objects is quite evident and well known to the world. because the pleasure which it affords is superior to the pleasure of the other kinds of love, which exists only for its sake.

What has been said in this chapter upon the subject of sexual union is sufficient for the learned; but for the edification of the ignorant, the same will now be treated of at length and in detail.

1 High unions are said to be better than low ones, for in the former it is
   possible for the male to satisfy his own passion without injuring the
   female, while in the latter it is difficult for the female to be satisfied by
   any means.

2 This paragraph should be particularly noted, for it specially applies to
   married men and their wives. So many men utterly ignore the feelings
   of the women, and never pay the slightest attention to the passion of the
   latter. To understand the subject thoroughly, it is absolutely necessary
   to study it, and then a person will know that, as dough is prepared for
   baking, so must a woman be prepared for sexual intercourse, if she is to
   derive satisfaction from it.

CHAPTER 2

ON THE EMBRACE

THIS PART OF THE *KAMA SHASTRA*, which treats of sexual union, is also called 'Sixty-four' (*Chatushshashti*). Some old authors say that it is called so, because it contains sixty-four chapters. The followers of Babhravya say on the other hand that this part contains eight subjects, viz. the embrace, kissing, scratching with the nails or fingers, biting, lying down, making various sounds, playing the part of a man, and the *Auparishtaka*, or mouth congress. Each of these subjects being of eight kinds, and eight multiplied by eight being sixty-four, this part is therefore named 'sixty-four'. But Vatsyayana affirms that as this part contains also the following subjects, viz. striking, crying, the acts of a man during congress, the various kinds of congress, and other subjects, the name 'sixty-four' is given to it only accidentally.

However the part sixty-four is now treated of, and the embrace, being the first subject, will now be considered.

Now the embrace which indicates the mutual love of a man and woman who have come together is of four kinds:

- Touching
- Rubbing
- Piercing
- Pressing

The action in each case is denoted by the meaning of the word which stands for it.

When a man under some pretext or other goes in front or alongside of a woman and touches her body with his own, it is called the 'touching embrace'. When a woman in a lonely place bends down, as if to pick up something, and pierces, as it were, a man sitting or standing, with her breasts, and the man in return takes hold of them, it is called a 'piercing embrace'.

The above two kinds of embrace take place only between persons who do not, as yet, speak freely with each other.

When two lovers are walking slowly together, either in the dark, or in a place of public resort, or in a lonely place, and rub their bodies against each other, it is called a 'rubbing embrace'.

When on the above occasion one of them presses the other's body forcibly against a wall or pillar, it is called a 'pressing embrace'.

These two last embraces are peculiar to those who know the intentions of each other.

At the time of the meeting the four following kinds of embrace are used:

- *Jataveshtitaka*, or the twining of a creeper.
- *Vrikshadhirudhaka*, or climbing a tree.
- *Tila-Tandulaka*, or the mixture of sesamum seed with rice.
- *Kshiraniraka*, or milk and water embrace.

When a woman, clinging to a man as a creeper twines round a tree, bends his head down to hers with the desire of kissing him and slightly makes the sound of '*sut sut*', embraces him, and looks lovingly towards him, it is called an embrace like the 'twining of a creeper'.

When a woman, having placed one of her feet on the foot of her lover, and the other on one of his thighs, passes one of her arms round his back, and the other on his shoulders, makes slightly the sounds of singing and cooing, and wishes, as it were, to climb up him in order to have a kiss, it is called an embrace like the 'climbing of a tree'.

These two kinds of embrace take place when the lover is standing.

When lovers lie on a bed, and embrace each other so closely that the arms and thighs of the one are encircled by the arms and thighs of the other, and are, as it were, rubbing up against them, this is called an embrace like 'the mixture of sesamum seed with rice'.

When a man and a woman are very much in love with each other, and, not thinking of any pain or hurt, embrace each other as if they were entering into each other's bodies either while the woman is sitting on the lap of the man, or in front of him, or on a bed, then it is called an embrace like a 'mixture of milk and water'.

These two kinds of embrace take place at the time of sexual union. Babhravya has thus related to us the above eight kinds of embraces.

Suvarnanabha moreover gives us four ways of embracing simple members of the body, which are:

- The embrace of the thighs.
- The embrace of the *jaghana*, i.e. the part of the body from the navel downwards to the thighs.

❧ The embrace of the breasts.

❧ The embrace of the forehead.

When one of two lovers presses forcibly one or both of the thighs of the other between his or her own, it is called the 'embrace of thighs'.

When a man presses the *jaghana* or middle part of the woman's body against his own, and mounts upon her to practise, either scratching with the nail or finger, or biting, or striking, or kissing, the hair of the woman being loose and flowing, it is called the 'embrace of the *jaghana*'.

When a man places his breast between the breasts of a woman and presses her with it, it is called the 'embrace of the breasts'.

When either of the lovers touches the mouth, the eyes and the forehead of the other with his or her own, it is called the 'embrace of the forehead'.

Some say that even shampooing is a kind of embrace, because there is a touching of bodies in it. But Vatsyayana thinks that shampooing is performed at a different time, and for a different purpose, and it is also of a different character, it cannot be said to be included in the embrace.

There are also some verses on the subject as follows:

'The whole subject of embracing is of such a nature that men who ask questions about it, or who hear about it, or who talk about it, acquire thereby a desire for enjoyment. Even those embraces that are not mentioned in the Kama Shastra *should be practised at the time of sexual enjoyment, if they are in any way conducive to the increase of love or passion. The rules of the* Shastra *apply so long as the passion of man is middling, but when the wheel of love is once set in motion, there is then no* Shastra *and no order.'*

CHAPTER 3

ON KISSING

IT IS SAID BY SOME that there is no fixed time or order between the embrace, the kiss, and the pressing or scratching with the nails or fingers, but that all these things should be done generally before sexual union takes place, while striking and making the various sounds generally takes place at the time of the union. Vatsyayana, however, thinks that anything may take place at any time, for love does not care for time or order.

On the occasion of the first congress, kissing and the other things mentioned above should be done moderately, they should not be continued for a long time, and should be done alternately. On subsequent occasions, however, the reverse of all this may take place, and moderation will not be necessary, they may continue for a long time, and, for the purpose of kindling love, they may be all done at the same time.

The following are the places for kissing: the forehead, the eyes, the cheeks, the throat, the bosom, the breasts, the lips, and the interior of the mouth. Moreover the people of the Lat country kiss also on the following places: the joints of the thighs, the arms and the navel. But Vatsyayana thinks that though kissing is practised by these people in the above places on account of the intensity of their love, and the customs of their country, it is not fit to be practised by all.

Now in a case of a young girl there are three sorts of kisses:
- The nominal kiss
- The throbbing kiss
- The touching kiss.

When a girl only touches the mouth of her lover with her own, but does not herself do anything, it is called the 'nominal kiss'.

When a girl, setting aside her bashfulness a little, wishes to touch the lip that is pressed into her mouth, and with that object moves her lower lip, but not the upper one, it is called the 'throbbing kiss'.

When a girl touches her lover's lip with her tongue, and having shut her eyes, places her hands on those of her lover, it is called the 'touching kiss'.

Other authors describe four other kinds of kisses:

- The straight kiss
- The bent kiss
- The turned kiss
- The pressed kiss.

When the lips of two lovers are brought into direct contact with each other, it is called a 'straight kiss'.

When the heads of two lovers are bent towards each other, and when so bent, kissing takes place, it is called a 'bent kiss'.

When one of them turns up the face of the other by holding the head and chin, and then kissing, it is called a 'turned kiss'.

Lastly when the lower lip is pressed with much force, it is called a 'pressed kiss'.

Kissing is of four kinds: moderate, contracted, pressed, and soft, according to the different parts of the body which are kissed, for different kinds of kisses are appropriate for different parts of the body.

When a woman looks at the face of her lover while he is asleep and kisses it to show her intention or desire, it is called a 'kiss that kindles love'.

When a woman kisses her lover while he is engaged in business, or while he is quarrelling with her, or while he is looking at something else, so that his mind may be turned away, it is called a 'kiss that turns away'.

When a lover coming home late at night kisses his beloved, who is asleep on her bed, in order to show her his desire, it is called a 'kiss that awakens'. On such an occasion the woman may pretend to be asleep at the time of her lover's arrival, so that she may know his intention and obtain respect from him.

When a person kisses the reflection of the person he loves in a mirror, in water, or on a wall, it is called a 'kiss showing the intention'.

When a person kisses a child sitting on his lap, or a picture, or an image, or figure, in the presence of the person beloved by him, it is called a 'transferred kiss'.

When at night at a theatre, or in an assembly of caste men, a man coming up to a woman kisses a finger of her hand if she be standing, or a toe of her foot if she be sitting, or when a woman is shampooing her lover's body, places her face on his thigh (as if she was sleepy) so as to inflame his passion, and kisses his thigh or great toe, it is called a 'demonstrative kiss'.

There is also a verse on this subject as follows:

'Whatever things may be done by one of the lovers to the other, the same should be returned by the other; that is, if the woman kisses him he should kiss her in return, if she strikes him he should also strike her in return.'

CHAPTER 4

ON PRESSING, OR MARKING, OR SCRATCHING WITH THE NAILS

WHEN LOVE BECOMES INTENSE, pressing with the nails or scratching the body with them is practised, and it is done on the following occasions: on the first visit; at the time of setting out on a journey; on the return from a journey; at the time when an angry lover is reconciled; and lastly when the woman is intoxicated.

But pressing with the nails is not a usual thing except with those who are intensely passionate, i.e. full of passion. It is employed, together with biting, by those to whom the practice is agreeable.

Pressing with the nails is of the eight following kinds, according to the forms of the marks which are produced:

- Sounding
- Half moon
- A circle
- A line
- A tiger's nail or claw
- A peacock's foot
- The jump of a hare
- The leaf of a blue lotus.

The places that are to be pressed with the nails are as follows: the arm pit, the throat, the breasts, the lips, the *jaghana*, or middle parts of the body, and the thighs. But Suvarnanabha is of opinion that when the impetuosity of passion is excessive, the places need not be considered.

The qualities of good nails are that they should be bright, well set, clean, entire, convex, soft, and glossy in appearance. Nails are of three kinds according to their size:

- Small
- Middling
- Large.

Large nails, which give grace to the hands, and attract the hearts of women from their appearance, are possessed by the Bengalees.

Small nails, which can be used in various ways, and are to be applied only with the object of giving pleasure, are possessed by the people of the southern districts.

Middling nails, which contain the properties of both the above kinds, belong to the people of the Maharashtra.

When a person presses the chin, the breasts, the lower lip, or the *jaghana* of another so softly that no scratch or mark is left, but only the hair on the body becomes erect from the touch of the nails, and the nails themselves make a sound, it is called a 'sounding or pressing with the nails'.

The curved mark with the nails, which is impressed on the neck and the breasts, is called the 'half moon'.

When the half moons are impressed opposite to each other, it is called a 'circle'. This mark with the nails is generally made on the navel, the small cavities about the buttocks, and on the joints of the thigh.

A mark in the form of a small line, and which can be made on any part of the body, is called a 'line'.

This same line, when it is curved, and made on the breast, is called a 'tiger's nail'.

When a curved mark is made on the breast by means of the five nails, it is called a 'peacock's foot'. This mark is made with the object of being praised, for it requires a great deal of skill to make it properly.

When five marks with the nails are made close to one another near the nipple of the breast, it is called 'the jump of a hare'.

A mark made on the breast or on the hips in the form of a leaf of the blue lotus is called the 'leaf of a blue lotus'.

When a person is going on a journey, and makes a mark on the thighs, or on the breast, it is called a 'token of remembrance'. On such an occasion three or four lines are impressed close to one another with the nails.

Here ends the marking with the nails. Marks of other kinds than the above may also be made with the nails, for the ancient authors say that, as there are innumerable degrees of skill among men (the practice of this art being known to all), so there are innumerable ways of making these marks. And as pressing or marking with the nails is independent of love, no one can say with certainty how many different kinds of marks with the nails do actually exist. The reason of this is, Vatsyayana says, that as variety is necessary in love, so love is to be produced by means of variety. It is on this account that courtesans, who are well acquainted with various ways and means, become so desirable, for if variety is sought in all the arts and amusements, such as archery and others, how much more should it be sought after in the present case.

There are also some verses on the subject, as follows:

'The love of a woman who sees the marks of nails on the private parts of her body, even though they are old and almost worn out, becomes again fresh and new. If there be no marks of nails to remind a person of the passages of love, then love is lessened in the same way as when no union takes place for a long time.'

CHAPTER 5

ON BITING

ALL THE PLACES THAT CAN be kissed are also the places that can be bitten, except the upper lip, the interior of the mouth, and the eyes.

The qualities of good teeth are as follows: they should be equal, possessed of a pleasing brightness, capable of being coloured, of proper proportions, unbroken, and with sharp ends.

The defects of teeth on the other hand are that they are blunt, protruding from the gums, rough, soft, large, and loosely set.

The following are the different kinds of biting:

- The hidden bite
- The swollen bite
- The point
- The line of points
- The coral and the jewel
- The line of jewels
- The broken cloud
- The biting of the boar.

The biting, which is shown only by the excessive redness of the skin that is bitten, is called the 'hidden bite'.

When the skin is pressed down on both sides, it is called the 'swollen bite'.

When a small portion of the skin is bitten with two teeth only, it is called the 'point'.

When such small portions of the skin are bitten with all the teeth, it is called the 'line of points'.

The biting, which is done by bringing together the teeth and the lips, is called the 'coral and the jewel'. The lip is the coral, and the teeth the jewel.

When biting is done with all the teeth, it is called the 'line of jewels'.

The biting, which consists of unequal risings in a circle, and which comes from the space between the teeth, is called the 'broken cloud'. This is impressed on the breasts.

The biting, which consists of many broad rows of marks near to one another, and with red intervals, is called the 'biting of a boar'. This is impressed on the breasts and the shoulders; and these two last modes of biting are peculiar to persons of intense passion.

The lower lip is the place on which the 'hidden bite', the 'swollen bite', and the 'point' are made; again the 'swollen bite' and the 'coral and the jewel' bite are done on the cheek. Kissing, pressing with the nails, and biting are the ornaments of the left cheek, and when the word cheek is used it is to be understood as the left cheek.

Both the 'line of points' and the 'line of jewels' are to be impressed on the throat, the arm pit, and the joints of the thighs; but the 'line of points' alone is to be impressed on the forehead and the thighs.

The marking with the nails, and the biting of the following things – an ornament of the forehead, an ear ornament, a bunch of flowers, a betel leaf, or a tamala leaf, which are worn by, or belong to the woman that is beloved – are signs of the desire of enjoyment.

Here end the different kinds of biting.

Among the things mentioned above, viz. embracing, kissing, etc., those which increase passion should be done first, and those which are only for amusement or variety should be done afterwards.

There are also some verses on this subject as follows:

'When a man bites a woman forcibly, she should angrily do the same to him with double force. Thus a "point" should be returned with a "line of points", and a "line of points" with a "broken cloud", and if she be excessively chafed, she should at once begin a love quarrel with him. At such a time she should take hold of her lover by the hair, and bend his head down, and kiss his lower lip, and then, being intoxicated with love, she should shut her eyes and bite him in various places. Even by day, and in a place of public resort, when her lover shows her any mark that she may have inflicted on his body, she should smile at the sight of it, and turning her face as if she were going to chide him, she should show him with an angry look the marks on her own body that have been made by him. Thus if men and women act according to each other's liking, their love for each other will not be lessened even in one hundred years.'

CHAPTER 6

ON THE DIFFERENT WAYS OF LYING DOWN, AND THE VARIOUS KINDS OF CONGRESS

ON THE OCCASION OF A 'HIGH CONGRESS' the *Mrigi* (Deer) woman should lie down in such a way as to widen her *yoni*, while in a 'low congress' the *Hastini* (Elephant) woman should lie down so as to contract hers. But in an 'equal congress' they should lie down in the natural position. What is said above concerning the *Mrigi* and the *Hastini* applies also to the *Vadawa* (Mare) woman. In a 'low congress' the woman should particularly make use of medicine, to cause her desires to be satisfied quickly.

The Deer-woman has the following three ways of lying down:
- The widely opened position
- The yawning position
- The position of the wife of Indra.

When she lowers her head and raises her middle parts, it is called the 'widely opened position'. At such a time the man should apply some unguent, so as to make the entrance easy.

When she raises her thighs and keeps them wide apart and engages in congress, it is called the 'yawning position'.

When she places her thighs with her legs doubled on them upon her sides, and thus engages in congress, it is called the position of Indrani and this is learnt only by practice. The position is also useful in the case of the 'highest congress'.

The 'clasping position' is used in 'low congress', and in the 'lowest congress', together with the 'pressing position', the 'twining position', and the 'mare's position'.

When the legs of both the male and the female are stretched straight out over each other, it is called the 'clasping position'. It is of two kinds, the side position and the supine position, according to the way in which they lie down. In the side position the male should invariably lie on his left side, and cause the woman to lie on her right side, and this rule is to be observed in lying down with all kinds of women.

When, after congress has begun in the clasping position, the woman presses her lover with her thighs, it is called the 'pressing position'.

When the woman places one of her thighs across the thigh of her lover it is called the 'twining position'.

When a woman forcibly holds in her *yoni* the *lingam* after it is in, it is called the 'mare's position'. This is learnt by practice only.

The above are the different ways of lying down, mentioned by Babhravya. Suvarnanabha, however, gives the following in addition:

When the female raises both of her thighs straight up, it is called the 'rising position'.

When she raises both of her legs, and places them on her lover's shoulders, it is called the 'yawning position'.

When the legs are contracted, and thus held by the lover before his bosom, it is called the 'pressed position'.

When only one of her legs is stretched out, it is called the 'half pressed position'.

When the woman places one of her legs on her lover's shoulder, and stretches the other out, and then places the latter on his shoulder, and stretches out the other, and continues to do so alternately, it is called the 'splitting of a bamboo'.

When one of her legs is placed on the head, and the other is stretched out, it is called the 'fixing of a nail'. This is learnt by practice only.

When both the legs of the woman are contracted, and placed on her stomach, it is called the 'crab's position'.

When the thighs are raised and placed one upon the other, it is called the 'packed position'.

When the shanks are placed one upon the other, it is called the 'lotus-like position'.

When a man, during congress, turns round, and enjoys the woman without leaving her, while she embraces him round the back all the time, it is called the 'turning position', and is learnt only by practice.

Thus, says Suvarnanabha, these different ways of lying down, sitting, and standing should be practised in water, because it is easy to do so therein. But Vatsyayana is of opinion that congress in water is improper, because it is prohibited by the religious law.

When a man and a woman support themselves on each other's bodies, or on a wall, or pillar, and thus while standing engage in congress, it is called the 'supported congress'.

When a man supports himself against a wall, and the woman, sitting on his hands joined together and held underneath her, throws her arms round his neck, and putting her thighs alongside his waist, moves herself by her feet, which are touching the wall against which the man is leaning, it is called the 'suspended congress'.

When a woman stands on her hands and feet like a quadruped, and her lover mounts her like a bull, it is called the 'congress of a cow'. At this time everything that is ordinarily done on the bosom should be done on the back.

In the same way can be carried on the congress of a dog, the congress of a goat, the congress of a deer, the forcible mounting of an ass, the congress of a cat, the jump of a tiger, the pressing of an elephant, the rubbing of a boar, and the mounting of a horse. And in all these cases the characteristics of these different animals should be manifested by acting like them.

When a man enjoys two women at the same time, both of whom love him equally, it is called the 'united congress'.

When a man enjoys many women altogether, it is called the 'congress of a herd of cows'.

The following kinds of congress, namely, sporting in water, or the congress of an elephant with many female elephants which is said to take place only in the water, the congress of a collection of goats, the congress of a collection of deer take place in imitation of these animals.

In Gramaneri many young men enjoy a woman that may be married to one of them, either one after the other, or at the same time. Thus one of them holds her, another enjoys her, a third uses her mouth, a fourth holds her middle part, and in this way they go on enjoying her several parts alternately.

The same things can be done when several men are sitting in company with one courtesan, or when one courtesan is alone with many men. In the same way this can be done by the women of the king's harem when they accidentally get hold of a man.

The people in the southern countries have also a congress in the anus, that is called the 'lower congress'.

Thus ends the various kinds of congress.

There is also a verse on the subject as follows:

'An ingenious person should multiply the kinds of congress after the fashion of the different kinds of beasts and of birds. For these different kinds of congress, performed according to the liking of each individual, generate love, friendship, and respect in the hearts of women.'

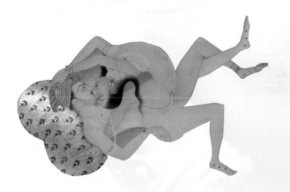

CHAPTER 7

ON THE VARIOUS WAYS OF STRIKING, AND ON THE SOUNDS APPROPRIATE TO THEM

SEXUAL INTERCOURSE CAN BE COMPARED to a quarrel, on account of the contrarieties of love and its tendency to dispute. The place of striking with passion is the body, and on the body the special places are:

- The shoulders
- The head
- The space between the breasts
- The back
- The *jaghana*, or middle part of the body
- The sides.

Striking is of four kinds:

- Striking with the back of the hand
- Striking with the fingers a little contracted
- Striking with the fist
- Striking with the open palm of the hand.

On account of its causing pain, striking gives rise to the hissing sound, which is of various kinds, and to the eight kinds of crying:

- The sound '*hin*'
- The thundering sound
- The cooing sound
- The weeping sound
- The sound '*phut*'
- The sound '*phât*'

🐦 The sound '*sût*'
🐦 The sound '*plât*'.

Besides these, there are also words having a meaning, such as 'mother', and those that are expressive of prohibition, sufficiency, desire of liberation, pain or praise, and to which may be added sounds like those of the dove, the cuckoo, the green pigeon, the parrot, the bee, the sparrow, the flamingo, the duck, and the quail, which are all occasionally made use of.

Blows with the fist should be given on the back of the woman while she is sitting on the lap of the man, and she should give blows in return, abusing the man as if she were angry, and making the cooing and the weeping sounds. While the woman is engaged in congress the space between the breasts should be struck with the back of the hand, slowly at first, and then proportionately to the increasing excitement, until the end.

At this time the sounds '*hin*' and others may be made, alternately or optionally, according to habit. When the man, making the sound '*phât*', strikes the woman on the head, with the fingers of his hand a little contracted, it is called *Prasritaka*, which means striking with the fingers of the hand a little contracted. In this case the appropriate sounds are the cooing sound, the sound '*phât*' and the sound '*phut*' in the interior of the mouth, and at the end of congress the sighing and weeping sounds. The sound '*phât*' is an imitation of the sound of a bamboo being split, while the sound '*phut*' is like the sound made by something falling into water. At all times when kissing and such like things are begun, the woman should give a reply with a hissing sound. During the excitement when the woman is not accustomed to striking, she continually utters words expressive of prohibition, sufficiency, or desire of liberation, as well as the words 'father', 'mother', intermingled with the sighing, weeping and thundering sounds.[1] Towards the conclusion of the congress, the breasts, the *jaghana*, and the sides of the woman should be pressed with the open palms of the hand, with some force, until the end of it, and then sounds like those of the quail or the goose should be made.

There are some verses on the subject as follows:

'*The characteristics of manhood are said to consist of roughness and impetuosity, while weakness, tenderness, sensibility, and an inclination to turn away from unpleasant things are the distinguishing marks of womanhood. The excitement of passion, and peculiarities of habit may sometimes cause contrary results to appear, but these do not last long, and in the end the natural state is resumed.*'

'About these things there cannot be either enumeration or any definite rule. Congress having once commenced, passion alone gives birth to all the acts of the parties.'

'Such passionate actions and amorous gesticulations or movements, which arise on the spur of the moment, and during sexual intercourse, cannot be defined, and are as irregular as dreams. A horse having once attained the fifth degree of motion goes on with blind speed, regardless of pits, ditches, and posts in his way; and in the same manner a loving pair become blind with passion in the heat of congress, and go on with great impetuosity, paying not the least regard to excess. For this reason one who is well acquainted with the science of love, and knowing his own strength, as also the tenderness, impetuosity, and strength of the young women, should act accordingly. The various modes of enjoyment are not for all times or for all persons, but they should only be used at the proper time and in the proper places.'

1 Men who are well acquainted with the art of love are well aware how often one woman differs from another in her sighs and sounds during the time of congress. Some women like to be talked to in the most loving way, others in the most lustful way, others in the most abusive way, and so on. Some women enjoy themselves with closed eyes in silence, others make a great noise over it, and some almost faint away. The great art is to ascertain what gives them the greatest pleasure, and what specialities they like best.

CHAPTER 8

ABOUT WOMEN ACTING THE PART OF A MAN; AND ON THE WORK OF A MAN

WHEN A WOMAN SEES THAT HER LOVER is fatigued by constant congress, without having his desire satisfied, she should, with his permission, lay him down upon his back, and give him assistance by acting his part. She may also do this to satisfy the curiosity of her lover, or her own desire of novelty.

There are two ways of doing this, the first is when during congress she turns round, and gets on the top of her lover, in such a manner as to continue the congress, without obstructing the pleasure of it; and the other is when she acts the man's part from the beginning. At such a time, with flowers in her hair hanging loose, and her smiles broken by hard breathings, she should press upon her lover's bosom with her own breasts, and lowering her head frequently, should do in return the same actions which he used to do before, returning his blows and chaffing him, should say, 'I was laid down by you, and fatigued with hard congress, I shall now therefore lay you down in return.' She should then again manifest her own bashfulness, her fatigue, and her desire of stopping the congress. In this way she should do the work of a man, which we shall presently relate.

Whatever is done by a man for giving pleasure to a woman is called the work of a man, and is as follows:

While the woman is lying on his bed, and is as it were abstracted by his conversation, he should loosen the knot of her undergarments, and when she begins to dispute with him, he should overwhelm her with kisses. Then when his *lingam* is erect he should touch her with his hands in various places, and gently manipulate various parts of the body. If the woman is bashful, and if it is the first time that they have come together, the man should place his hands between her thighs, which she would probably keep close together, and if she is a very young girl, he should first get his hands upon her breasts, which she would probably cover with her own hands, and under her armpits and on her neck. If however she is a seasoned woman, he should do whatever is agreeable either to him or to her, and whatever is fitting for the occasion. After this he should take hold of her hair, and hold her chin in his fingers for the purpose of kissing her. On this, if she is a young girl, she will become bashful and close her eyes. Anyhow he should gather from the action of the woman what things would be pleasing to her during congress.

Here Suvarnanabha says that while a man is doing to the woman what he likes best during congress, he should always make a point of pressing those parts of her body on which she turns her eyes.

The signs of the enjoyment and satisfaction of the woman are as follows: her body relaxes, she closes her eyes, she puts aside all bashfulness, and shows increased willingness to unite the two organs as closely together as possible. On the other hand, the signs of her want of enjoyment and of failing to be satisfied are as follows: she shakes her hands, she does not let the man get up, feels dejected, bites the man, kicks him, and continues to go on moving after the man has finished. In such cases the man should rub the *yoni* of the woman with his hand and fingers (as the elephant rubs anything with his trunk) before engaging in congress, until it is softened, and after that is done he should proceed to put his *lingam* into her.

The acts to be done by the man are:
- Moving forward
- Friction or churning
- Piercing
- Rubbing
- Pressing
- Giving a blow
- The blow of a boar
- The blow of a bull
- The sporting of a sparrow.

When the organs are brought together properly and directly it is called 'moving the organ forward'.

When the *lingam* is held with the hand, and turned all round in the *yoni*, it is called 'churning'.

When the *yoni* is lowered, and the upper part of it is struck with the *lingam*, it is called 'piercing'.

When the same thing is done on the lower part of the *yoni*, it is called 'rubbing'.

When the *yoni* is pressed by the *lingam* for a long time, it is called 'pressing'.

When the *lingam* is removed to some distance from the *yoni*, and then forcibly strikes it, it is called 'giving a blow'.

When only one part of the *yoni* is rubbed with the *lingam*, it is called the 'blow of a boar'.

When both sides of the *yoni* are rubbed in this way, it is called the 'blow of a bull'.

When the *lingam* is in the *yoni*, and moved up and down frequently, and without being taken out, it is called the 'sporting of a sparrow'. This takes place at the end of congress.

When a woman acts the part of a man, she has the following things to do in addition to the nine given above:

- The pair of tongs
- The top
- The swing.

When the woman holds the *lingam* in her *yoni*, draws it in, presses it, and keeps it thus in her for a long time, it is called the 'pair of tongs'.

When, while engaged in congress, she turns round like a wheel, it is called the 'top'. This is learnt by practice only.

When, on such an occasion, the man lifts up the middle part of his body, and the woman turns round her middle part, it is called the 'swing'.

When the woman is tired, she should place her forehead on that of her lover, and should thus take rest without disturbing the union of the organs, and when the woman has rested herself the man should turn round and begin the congress again.

There are also some verses on the subject as follows:

'Though a woman is reserved, and keeps her feelings concealed; yet when she gets on the top of a man, she then shows all her love and desire. A man should gather from the actions of the woman of what disposition she is, and in what way she likes to be enjoyed. A woman during her monthly courses, a woman who has been lately confined, and a fat woman should not be made to act the part of a man.'

CHAPTER 9

ON THE *AUPARISHTAKA* OR MOUTH CONGRESS

THERE ARE TWO KINDS OF EUNUCHS, those that are disguised as males, and those that are disguised as females. Eunuchs disguised as females imitate their dress, speech, gestures, tenderness, timidity, simplicity, softness and bashfulness. The acts that are done on the *jaghana* or middle parts of women, are done in the mouths of these eunuchs, and this is called *Auparishtaka*.[1] These eunuchs derive their imaginable pleasure, and their livelihood from this kind of congress, and they lead the life of courtesans. So much concerning eunuchs disguised as females.

Eunuchs disguised as males keep their desires secret, and when they wish to do anything they lead the life of shampooers. Under the pretence of shampooing, a eunuch of this kind embraces and draws towards himself the thighs of the man whom he is shampooing, and after this he touches the joints of his thighs and his *jaghana*, or central portions of his body. Then, if he finds the *lingam* of the man erect, he presses it with his hands and chaffs him for getting into that state. If after this, and after knowing his intention, the man does not tell the eunuch to proceed, then the latter does it of his own accord and begins the congress. If however he is ordered by the man to do it, then he disputes with him, and only consents at last with difficulty.

The following eight things are then done by the eunuch one after the other:

- The nominal congress
- Biting the sides
- Pressing outside
- Pressing inside

- Kissing
- Rubbing
- Sucking a mango fruit
- Swallowing up.

At the end of each of these, the eunuch expresses his wish to stop, but when one of them is finished, the man desires him to do another, and after that is done, then the one that follows it, and so on.

When, holding the man's *lingam* with his hand, and placing it between his lips, the eunuch moves about his mouth, it is called the 'nominal congress'.

When, covering the end of the *lingam* with his fingers collected together like the bud of a plant or flower, the eunuch presses the sides of it with his lips, using his teeth also, it is called 'biting the sides'.

When, being desired to proceed, the eunuch presses the end of the *lingam* with his lips closed together, and kisses it as if he were drawing it out, it is called the 'outside pressing'.

When, being asked to go on, he puts the *lingam* further into his mouth, and presses it with his lips and then takes it out, it is called the 'inside pressing'.

When, holding the *lingam* in his hand, the eunuch kisses it as if he were kissing the lower lip, it is called 'kissing'.

When, after kissing it, he touches it with his tongue everywhere, and passes the tongue over the end of it, it is called 'rubbing'.

When, in the same way, he puts the half of it into his mouth, and forcibly kisses and sucks it, this is called 'sucking a mango fruit'.

And lastly, when, with the consent of the man, the eunuch puts the whole *lingam* into his mouth, and presses it to the very end, as if he were going to swallow it up, it is called 'swallowing up'.

Striking, scratching, and other things may also be done during this kind of congress.

The *Auparishtaka* is practised also by unchaste and wanton women, female attendants and serving maids, i.e. those who are not married to anybody, but who live by shampooing.

There are also the following verses on the subject:

'The male servants of some men carry on the mouth congress with their masters. It is also practised by some citizens, who know each other well, among themselves. Some women of the harem, when they are amorous, do the acts of the mouth on the yonis *of one another, and some men do the same thing with women. The way of doing this (i.e. of kissing the* yoni*) should be known*

from kissing the mouth. When a man and woman lie down in an inverted order, i.e. with the head of the one towards the feet of the other and carry on this congress, it is called the "congress of a crow".'

1 This practice appears to have been prevalent in some parts of India from a very ancient time. The *Shustruta*, a work on medicine some two thousand years old, describes the wounding of the *lingam* with the teeth as one of the causes of a disease treated upon in that work.

CHAPTER 10

On how to begin and how to end the congress. Different kinds of congress and love quarrels

IN THE PLEASURE-ROOM, DECORATED with flowers, and fragrant with perfumes, attended by his friends and servants, the citizen should receive the woman, who will come bathed and dressed, and will invite her to take refreshment and to drink freely. He should then seat her on his left side, and holding her hair, and touching also the end and knot of her garment, he should gently embrace her with his right arm. They should then carry on an amusing conversation on various subjects, and may also talk suggestively of things which would be considered as coarse, or not to be mentioned generally in society. They may then sing, either with or without gesticulations, and play on musical instruments, talk about the arts, and persuade each other to drink. At last when the woman is overcome with love and desire, the citizen should dismiss the people that may be with him, giving them flowers, ointments, and betel leaves, and then when the two are left alone, they should proceed as has been already described in the previous chapters.

Such is the beginning of sexual union. At the end of the congress, the lovers with modesty, and not looking at each other, should go separately to the washing-room. After this, sitting in their own places, they should eat some betel leaves, and the citizen should apply with his own hand to the body of the woman some pure sandal wood ointment, or ointment of some other kind. He should then embrace her with his left arm, and with agreeable words should cause her to drink from a cup held in his own hand, or he may give her water to drink. They can then eat sweetmeats, or anything else, according to their likings and may drink fresh juice, soup, gruel, extracts of meat, sherbet, the juice of mango fruits, the extract of the juice of the citron tree mixed with sugar, or anything known to be sweet, soft, and pure. The lovers may also sit on the terrace of the palace or house, and enjoy the moonlight, and carry on an agreeable conversation. At this time, too, while the woman lies in his lap, with her face towards the moon, the citizen should show her the different planets, the morning star, the polar star, and the seven Rishis, or Great Bear.

This is the end of sexual union.

Congress is of the following kinds:
- Loving congress
- Congress of subsequent love
- Congress of artificial love
- Congress of transferred love
- Congress like that of eunuchs
- Deceitful congress
- Congress of spontaneous love.

When a man and a woman, who have been in love with each other for some time, come together with great difficulty, or when one of the two returns from a journey, or is reconciled after having been separated on account of a quarrel, then congress is called the 'loving congress'. It is carried on according to the liking of the lovers, and as long as they choose.

When two persons come together, while their love for each other is still in its infancy, their congress is called the 'congress of subsequent love'.

When a man carries on the congress by exciting himself by means of the sixty-four ways, such as kissing, etc., etc., or when a man and a woman come together, though in reality they are both attached to different persons, their congress is then called 'congress of artificial love'. At this time all the ways and means mentioned in the *Kama Shastra* should be used.

When a man, from the beginning to the end of the congress, though having connection with the woman, thinks all the time that he is enjoying another one whom he loves, it is called the 'congress of transferred love'.

Congress between a man and a female water carrier, or a female servant of a caste lower than his own, lasting only until the desire is satisfied, is called 'congress like that of eunuchs'. Here external touches, kisses, and manipulation are not to be employed.

The congress between a courtesan and a rustic, and that between citizens and the women of villages, and bordering countries, is called 'deceitful congress'.

The congress that takes place between two persons who are attached to one another, and which is done according to their own liking is called 'spontaneous congress'.

Thus end the kinds of congress.

WE SHALL NOW SPEAK OF LOVE QUARRELS.

A woman who is very much in love with a man cannot bear to hear the name of her rival mentioned, or to have any conversation regarding her, or to be addressed by her name through mistake. If such takes place, a great quarrel arises, and the woman cries, becomes angry, tosses her hair about, strikes her lover, falls from her bed or seat, and, casting aside her garlands and ornaments, throws herself down on the ground.

At this time, the lover should attempt to reconcile her with conciliatory words, and should take her up carefully and place her on her bed. But she, not replying to his questions, and with increased anger, should bend down his head by pulling his hair, and having kicked him once, twice, or thrice on his arms, head, bosom or back, should then proceed to the door of the room. Dattaka says that she should then sit angrily near the door and shed tears, but should not go out, because she would be found fault with for going away. After a time, when she thinks that the conciliatory words and actions of her lover have reached their utmost, she should then embrace him, talking to him with harsh and reproachful words, but at the same time showing a loving desire for congress.

When the woman is in her own house, and has quarrelled with her lover, she should go to him and show how angry she is, and leave him. Afterwards the citizen having sent the *Vita*, the *Vidushaka* or the *Pithamarda*[1] to pacify her, she should accompany them back to the house, and spend the night with her lover.

Thus end the love quarrels.

IN CONCLUSION.

A man, employing the sixty-four means mentioned by Babhravya, obtains his object, and enjoys the woman of the first quality. Though he may speak well on other subjects, if he does not know the sixty-four divisions, no great respect is paid to him in the assembly of the learned. A man, devoid of other knowledge, but well acquainted with the sixty-four divisions, becomes a leader in any society of men and women. What man will not respect the sixty-four arts,[2] considering they are respected by the learned, by the cunning, and by the courtesans. As the sixty-four arts are respected, are charming, and add to the talent of women, they are called by the *Acharyas* dear to women. A man skilled in the sixty-four arts is looked upon with love by his own wife, by the wives of others, and by courtesans.

1 The characteristics of these three individuals have been given in Part One, Chapter 4, page 29.

2 A definition of the sixty-four arts is given in Part One, Chapter 3, pages 21–23.

PART THREE

ABOUT THE ACQUISITION OF A WIFE

ON MARRIAGE

WHEN A GIRL OF THE SAME CASTE, and a virgin, is married in accordance with the precepts of Holy Writ, the results of such a union are the acquisition of *Dharma* and *Artha*, offspring, affinity, increase of friends, and untarnished love. For this reason a man should fix his affections upon a girl who is of good family, whose parents are alive, and who is three years or more younger than himself. She should be born of a highly respectable family, possessed of wealth, well connected, and with many relations and friends. She should also be beautiful, of a good disposition, with lucky marks on her body, and with good hair, nails, teeth, ears, eyes and breasts, neither more nor less than they ought to be, and no one of them entirely wanting, and not troubled with a sickly body. The man should, of course, also possess these qualities himself. But at all events, says Ghotakamukha, a girl who has been already joined with others (i.e. no longer a maiden) should never be loved, for it would be reproachable to do such a thing.

Now in order to bring about a marriage with such a girl as described above, the parents and relations of the man should exert themselves, as also such friends on both sides as may be desired to assist in the matter. These friends should bring to the notice of the girl's parents, the faults, both present and future, of all the other men that may wish to marry her, and should at the same time extol even to exaggeration all the excellencies, ancestral, and paternal, of their friend, so as to endear him to them, and particularly to those that may be liked by the girl's mother. One of the friends should also disguise himself as an astrologer, and declare the future good fortune and wealth of his friend by showing the existence of all the lucky omens and signs, the good influence of planets, the auspicious entrance of the sun into a sign of the Zodiac, propitious stars and fortunate marks on his body. Others again should rouse the jealousy of the girl's mother by telling her that their friend has a chance of getting from some other quarter even a better girl than hers.

A girl should be taken as a wife, as also given in marriage, when fortune, signs, omens, and the words of others are favourable, for, says Ghotakamukha, a man should not marry at any time he likes. A girl who is asleep, crying, or gone out of the house when sought in marriage, or who is betrothed to another, should not be married.

Some authors say that prosperity is gained only by marrying that girl to whom one becomes attached, and that therefore no other girl but the one who is loved should be married by anyone.

When a girl becomes marriageable her parents should dress her smartly, and should place her where she can be easily seen by all. Every afternoon, having dressed her and decorated her in a becoming manner, they should send her with her female companions to sports, sacrifices, and marriage ceremonies, and thus show her to advantage in society, because she is a kind of merchandise. They should also receive with kind words and signs of friendliness those of an auspicious appearance who may come accompanied by their friends and relations for the purpose of marrying their daughter, and under some pretext or other having first dressed her becomingly, should then present her to them. After this they should await the pleasure of fortune, and with this object should appoint a future day on which a determination could be come to with regard to their daughter's marriage. On this occasion when the persons have come, the parents of the girl should ask them to bathe and dine, and should say, 'Everything will take place at the proper time', and should not then comply with the request, but should settle the matter later.

When a girl is thus acquired, either according to the custom of the country, or according to his own desire, the man should marry her in accordance with the precepts of the Holy Writ, according to one of the four kinds of marriage.

Thus ends marriage.

There are also some verses on the subject as follows:

'Amusement in society, such as completing verses begun by others, marriages, and auspicious ceremonies should be carried on neither with superiors, nor inferiors, but with our equals. That should be known as a high connection when a man, after marrying a girl, has to serve her and her relations afterwards like a servant, and such a connection is censured by the good. On the other hand, that reproachable connection, where a man, together with his relations, lords it over his wife, is called a low connection by the wise. But when both the man and the woman afford mutual pleasure to each other, and when the relatives on both sides

pay respect to one another, such is called a connection in the proper sense of the word. Therefore a man should contract neither a high connection by which he is obliged to bow down afterwards to his kinsmen, nor a low connection, which is universally reprehended by all.'

CHAPTER 2

ON CREATING CONFIDENCE
IN THE GIRL

FOR THE FIRST THREE DAYS after marriage, the girl and her husband should sleep on the floor, abstain from sexual pleasures, and eat their food without seasoning it either with alkali or salt. For the next seven days they should bathe amidst the sounds of auspicious musical instruments, should decorate themselves, dine together, and pay attention to their relations as well as to those who may have come to witness their marriage. This is applicable to persons of all castes. On the night of the tenth day the man should begin in a lonely place with soft words, and thus create confidence in the girl. Women, being of a tender nature, want tender beginnings, and when they are forcibly approached by men with whom they are but slightly acquainted, they sometimes suddenly become haters of sexual connection, and sometimes even haters of the male sex. The man should therefore approach the girl according to her liking, and should make use of those devices by which he may be able to establish himself more and more into her confidence. These devices are as follows:

He should embrace her first of all in a way she likes most, because it does not last for a long time.

He should embrace her with the upper part of his body because that is easier and simpler. If the girl is grown up, or if the man has known her for some time, he may embrace her by the light of a lamp, but if he is not well acquainted with her, or if she is a young girl, he should then embrace her in darkness.

When the girl accepts the embrace, the man should put a tambula or screw of betel nut and betel leaves in her mouth, and if she will not take it, he should induce her to do so by conciliatory words, entreaties, oaths, and kneeling at her feet, for it is a universal rule that however bashful or angry a woman may be she never disregards a man's kneeling at her feet. At the time of giving this tambula he should kiss her mouth softly and gracefully without making any sound. When she is gained over in this respect he should then make her talk, and so that she may be induced to talk he should ask her questions about things of which he knows or pretends to know nothing, and which can be answered in a few words. If she does not speak to him, he should not frighten her, but should ask her the same thing again and again in a conciliatory manner. If she does not then speak he should urge her to give a reply because, as Ghotakamukha says, 'all girls hear everything said to them by men, but do not themselves sometimes say a single word'. When she is thus importuned, the girl should give replies by shakes of the head, but if she has quarrelled with the man she should not even do that. When she is asked by the man whether she wishes for him, and whether she likes him, she should remain silent for a long time, and when at last importuned to reply, should give him a favourable answer by a nod of her head. If the man is previously acquainted with the girl he should converse with her by means of a female friend, who may be favourable to him, and in the confidence of both, and carry on the conversation on both sides. On such an occasion the girl should smile with her head bent down, and if the female friend say more on her part than she was desired to do, she should chide her and dispute with her. The female friend should say in jest even what she is not desired to say by the girl, and add, 'she says so', on which the girl should say indistinctly and prettily, 'O no! I did not say so', and she should then smile and throw an occasional glance towards the man.

If the girl is familiar with the man, she should place near him, without saying anything, the tambula, the ointment, or the garland that he may have asked for, or she may tie them up in his upper garment. While she is engaged in this, the man should touch her young breasts in the sounding way of pressing with the nails, and if she prevents him doing this he should say to her, ' I will not do it again if you will embrace me', and should in this way cause her to embrace him. While he is being embraced by her he should pass his hand repeatedly over and about her body. By and by he should place her in his lap, and try more and more to gain her consent, and if she will not yield to him he should frighten her by saying 'I shall impress marks of my teeth and nails on your lips and breasts, and then make similar marks on my own body, and shall tell my friends that you did them. What will you say then?' In this and other ways, as fear and confidence are created in the minds of children, so should the man gain her over to his wishes.

On the second and third nights, after her confidence has increased still more, he should feel the whole of her body with his hands, and kiss her all over; he should also place his hands upon her thighs and shampoo them, and if he succeed in this he should then shampoo the joints of her thighs. If she tries to prevent him doing this he should say to her, 'What harm is there in doing it?' and should persuade her to let him do it. After gaining this point he should touch her private parts, should loosen her girdle and the knot of her dress, and turning up her lower garment should shampoo the joints of her naked thighs. Under various pretences he should do all these things, but he should not at that time begin actual congress. After this he should teach her the sixty-four arts, should tell her how much he loves her, and describe to her the hopes which he formerly entertained regarding her. He should also promise to be faithful to her in future, and should dispel all her fears with respect to rival women, and, at last, after having overcome her bashfulness, he should begin to enjoy her in a way so as not to frighten her. So much about creating confidence in the girl; and there are, moreover, some verses on the subject as follows:

'A man acting according to the inclinations of a girl should try to gain her over so that she may love him and place her confidence in him. A man does not succeed either by implicitly following the inclination of a girl, or by wholly opposing her, and he should therefore adopt a middle course. He who knows how to make himself beloved by women, as well as to increase their honour and create confidence in them, this man becomes an object of their love. But he who neglects a girl, thinking she is too bashful, is despised by her as a beast ignorant of the working of the female mind. Moreover, a girl forcibly enjoyed by one who does not understand the hearts of girls becomes nervous, uneasy, and dejected, and suddenly begins to hate the man who has taken advantage of her; and then, when her love is not understood or returned, she sinks into despondency, and becomes either a hater of mankind altogether, or, hating her own man, she has recourse to other men.'

CHAPTER 3

ON COURTSHIP, AND THE MANIFESTATION OF THE FEELINGS BY OUTWARD SIGNS AND DEEDS

A POOR MAN POSSESSED OF GOOD QUALITIES, a man born of a low family possessed of mediocre qualities, a neighbour possessed of wealth, and one under the control of his father, mother or brothers, should not marry without endeavouring to gain over the girl from her childhood to love and esteem him. Thus a boy separated from his parents, and living in the house of his uncle, should try to gain over the daughter of his uncle, or some other girl, even though she be previously betrothed to another. And this way of gaining over a girl, says Ghotakamukha, is unexceptional, because *Dharma* can be accomplished by means of it as well as by any other way of marriage.

When a boy has thus begun to woo the girl he loves, he should spend his time with her and amuse her with various games and diversions fitted for their age and acquaintanceship. In addition to this, he should carry on various amusing games played by several persons together, such as hide and seek, blindman's buff, gymnastic exercises, and other games of the same sort, in company with the girl, her friends and female attendants. The man should also show great kindness to any woman whom the girl thinks fit to be trusted, and should also make new acquaintances, but above all he should attach to himself by kindness and little services the daughter of the girl's nurse, for if she be gained over, even though she comes to know of his design, she does not cause any obstruction, but is sometimes even able to effect a union between him and the girl. And though she knows the true character of the man, she always talks of his many excellent qualities to the parents and relations of the girl, even though she may not be desired to do so by him.

In this way the man should do whatever the girl takes most delight in, and he should get for her whatever she may have a desire to possess. Thus he should procure for her such playthings as may be hardly known to other girls. Such things should be given at different times whenever he gets a good opportunity of meeting her, and some of them should be given in private, and some in public, according to circumstances. In short, he should try in every way to make her look upon him as one who would do for her everything that she wanted to be done.

In the next place he should get her to meet him in some place privately, and should then tell her that the reason of his giving presents to her in secret was the fear that the parents of both of them might be displeased, and then he may add that the things which he had given her had been much desired by other people. When her love begins to show signs of increasing he should relate to her agreeable stories if she expresses a wish to hear such narratives. Or if she takes delight in legerdemain, he should amaze her by performing various tricks of jugglery; or if she feels a great curiosity to see a performance of the various arts, he should show his own skill in them. When she is delighted with singing he should entertain her with music, and on certain days, and at the time of going together to moonlight fairs and festivals, and at the time of her return after being absent from home, he should present her with bouquets of flowers, and with chaplets for the head, and with ear ornaments and rings, for these are the proper occasions on which such things should be presented.

He should also teach the daughter of the girl's nurse all the sixty-four means of pleasure practised by men, and under this pretext should also inform her of his great skill in the art of sexual enjoyment. All this time he should wear a fine dress, and make as good an appearance as possible, for young women love men who live with them, and who are handsome, good looking and well dressed. As for the sayings that though women may fall in love, they still make no effort themselves to gain over the object of their affections, that is only a matter of idle talk.

Now a girl always shows her love by outward signs and actions, such as the following:

She never looks the man in the face, and becomes abashed when she is looked at by him; under some pretext or other she shows her limbs to him; she looks secretly at him though he has gone away from her side, hangs down her head when she is asked some question by him, and answers in indistinct words and unfinished sentences, delights to be in his company for a long time, speaks to her attendants in a peculiar tone with the hope of attracting his attention towards her when she is at a distance from him, does not wish to go from the place where he is, under some pretext or other she makes him look at different things, narrates to him tales and stories very slowly so that she may continue conversing with him for a long time, kisses and embraces before him a child sitting in her lap, draws ornamental marks on the foreheads of her female servants, performs sportive and graceful movements when her attendants speak jestingly to her in the presence of her lover, confides in her lover's friends, and respects and obeys them, shows kindness to his servants, converses with them, and engages them to do her work as if she were their mistress, and listens attentively to them when they tell stories about her lover to somebody else, enters his house when induced to do so by the daughter of her nurse, and by her assistance manages to converse and play with him, avoids being seen by her lover when she is not dressed and decorated, gives him by the hand of her female friend her ear ornament, ring, or garland of flowers that he may have asked to see, always wears anything that he may have presented to her, becomes dejected when any other bridegroom is mentioned by her parents, and does not mix with those who may be of his party, or who may support his claims.

There are also some verses on the subject as follows:

'A man, who has seen and perceived the feelings of the girl towards him, and who has noticed the outward signs and movements by which those feelings are expressed, should do everything in his power to effect a union with her. He should gain over a young girl by childlike sports, a damsel come of age by his skill in the arts, and a girl that loves him by having recourse to persons in whom she confides.'

On things to be done only by the man, and the acquisition of the girl thereby. Also what is to be done by a girl to gain over a man and subject him to her

NOW WHEN THE GIRL BEGINS to show her love by outward signs and motions, as described in the last chapter, the lover should try to gain her over entirely by various ways and means, such as the following:

When engaged with her in any game or sport he should intentionally hold her hand. He should practise upon her the various kinds of embraces, such as the touching embrace, and others already described in a preceding chapter (Part Two, Chapter 2). When engaged in water sports, he should dive at a distance from her, and come up close to her.

He should describe to her the pangs he suffers on her account. He should relate to her the beautiful dream that he has had with reference to other women. At parties and assemblies of his caste he should sit near her, and touch her under some pretence or other, and having placed his foot upon hers, he should slowly touch each of her toes, and press the ends of the nails; if successful in this, he should get hold of her foot with his hand and repeat the same thing. He should also press a finger of her hand between his toes when she happens to be washing his feet; and whenever he gives anything to her or takes anything from her, he should show her by his manner and look how much he loves her.

Whenever he sits with her on the same seat or bed he should say to her, 'I have something to tell you in private', and then, when she comes to hear it in a quiet place, he should express his love to her more by manner and signs than by words. When he comes to know the state of her feelings towards him he should pretend to be ill, and should make her come to his house to speak to him. There he should intentionally hold her hand and place it on his eyes and forehead, and under the pretence of preparing some medicine for him he should ask her to do the work for his sake in the following words: 'This work must be done by you, and by nobody else.' When she wants to go away he should let her go, with an earnest request to come and see him again. This device of illness should be continued for three days and three nights. After this, when she begins coming to see him frequently, he should carry on long conversations with her, for, says Ghotakamukha, 'though a man loves a girl ever so much, he never succeeds in winning her without a great deal of talking'. At last, when the man finds the girl completely gained over, he may then begin to enjoy her. As for the saying that women grow less timid than usual during the evening, and in darkness, and are desirous of congress at those times, and do not oppose men then, and should only be enjoyed at these hours, it is a matter of talk only.

At last, when he knows the state of her feelings by her outward manner and conduct towards him at religious ceremonies, marriage ceremonies, fairs, festivals, theatres, public assemblies, and such like occasions, he should begin to enjoy her when she is alone, for Vatsyayana lays it down, that women, when resorted to at proper times and in proper places, do not turn away from their lovers.

When a girl, possessed of good qualities and well-bred, though born in a humble family, or destitute of wealth, and not therefore desired by her equals, or an orphan girl, or one deprived of her parents, but observing the rules of her family and caste, should wish to bring about her own marriage when she comes of age, such a girl should endeavour

to gain over a strong and good looking young man, or a person whom she thinks would marry her on account of the weakness of his mind, and even without the consent of his parents. She should do this by such means as would endear her to the said person, as well as by frequently seeing and meeting him. Her mother also should constantly cause them to meet by means of her female friends, and the daughter of her nurse. The girl herself should try to get alone with her beloved in some quiet place, and at odd times should give him flowers, betel nut, betel leaves and perfumes. She should also show her skill in the practice of the arts, in shampooing, in scratching and in pressing with the nails. She should also talk to him on the subjects he likes best, and discuss with him the ways and means of gaining over and winning the affections of a girl.

But old authors say that although the girl loves the man ever so much, she should not offer herself, or make the first overtures, for a girl who does this loses her dignity, and is liable to be scorned and rejected. But when the man shows his wish to enjoy her, she should be favourable to him and should show no change in her demeanour when he embraces her, and should receive all the manifestations of his love as if she were ignorant of the state of his mind. But when he tries to kiss her she should oppose him; when he begs to be allowed to have sexual intercourse with her she should let him touch her private parts only and with considerable difficulty; and though importuned by him, she should not yield herself up to him as if of her own accord, but should resist his attempts to have her. It is only, moreover, when she is certain that she is truly loved, and that her lover is indeed devoted to her, and will not change his mind, that she should then give herself up to him, and persuade him to marry her quickly. After losing her virginity she should tell her confidential friends about it.

Here end the efforts of a girl to gain over a man.

There are also some verses on the subject as follows:

'A girl who is much sought after should marry the man that she likes, and whom she thinks would be obedient to her, and capable of giving her pleasure. But when from the desire of wealth a girl is married by her parents to a rich man without taking into consideration the character or looks of the bridegroom, or when given to a man who has several wives, she never becomes attached to the man, even though he be endowed with good qualities, obedient to her will, active, strong, and healthy, and anxious to please her in every way. A husband who is obedient but yet master of himself, though he be poor and not good looking, is better than one who is common to many women, even though he be handsome and attractive.*

104

A man who is of a low mind, who has fallen from his social position, and who is much given to travelling, does not deserve to be married; neither does one who has many wives and children, or one who is devoted to sport and gambling, and who comes to his wife only when he likes. Of all the lovers of a girl he only is her true husband who possesses the qualities that are liked by her, and such a husband only enjoys real superiority over her, because he is the husband of love.'

CHAPTER 5

ON CERTAIN FORMS OF MARRIAGE[1]

WHEN A GIRL CANNOT MEET HER LOVER frequently in private, she should send the daughter of her nurse to him, it being understood that she has confidence in her, and had previously gained her over to her interests. On seeing the man, the daughter of the nurse should, in the course of conversation, describe to him the noble birth, the good disposition, the beauty, talent, skill, knowledge of human nature and affection of the girl in such a way as not to let him suppose that she had been sent by the girl, and should thus create affection for the girl in the heart of the man. To the girl also she should speak about the excellent qualities of the man, especially of those qualities which she knows are pleasing to the girl. She should, moreover, speak with disparagement of the other lovers of the girl, and talk about the avarice and indiscretion of their parents, and the fickleness of their relations. She should also quote samples of many girls of ancient times, such as Sakoontala and others, who, having united themselves with lovers of their own caste and their own choice, were ever happy afterwards in their society. And she should also tell of other girls who married into great families, and being troubled by rival wives, became wretched and miserable, and were finally abandoned. She should further speak of the good fortune, the continual happiness, the chastity, obedience, and affection of the man, and if the girl gets amorous about him, she should endeavour to allay her shame and her fear as well as her suspicions about any disaster that might result from her marriage. In a word, she should act the whole part of a female messenger by telling the girl all about the man's affection for her, the places he frequented, and the endeavours he made to meet her.

THE FORMS OF MARRIAGE

When the girl is gained over, and acts openly with the man as his wife, he should cause fire to be brought from the house of a *Brahman*, and having spread the Kusha grass upon the ground, and offered an oblation to the fire, he should marry her according to the precepts of the religious law. After this he should inform his parents of the fact, because it is the opinion of ancient authors that a marriage solemnly contracted in the presence of fire cannot afterwards be set aside.

After the consummation of the marriage, the relations of the man should gradually be made acquainted with the affair, and the relations of the girl should also be apprised of it in such a way that they may consent to the marriage, and overlook the manner in which it was brought about, and when this is done they should afterwards be reconciled by affectionate presents and favourable conduct. In this manner the man should marry the girl according to the Gandharva form of marriage.[2]

When the girl cannot make up her mind, or will not express her readiness to marry, the man should obtain her in any one of the following ways:

On a fitting occasion, and under some excuse, he should, by means of a female friend with whom he is well acquainted, and whom he can trust, and who also is well known to the girl's family, get the girl brought unexpectedly to his house, and he should then bring fire from the house of a *Brahman*, and proceed as before described.

When the marriage of the girl with some other person draws near, the man should disparage the future husband to the utmost in the mind of the mother of the girl, and then having got the girl to come with her mother's consent to a neighbouring house, he should bring fire from the house of a *Brahman*, and proceed as above.

The man should become a great friend of the brother of the girl, the said brother being of the same age as himself, and addicted to courtesans, and to intrigues with the wives of other people, and should give him assistance in such matters, and also give him occasional presents. He should then tell him about his great love for his sister, as young men will sacrifice even their lives for the sake of those who may be of the same age, habits, and dispositions as themselves. After this the man should get the girl brought by means of her brother to some secure place, and having brought fire from the house of a *Brahman* should proceed as before.

There are verses on this subject as follows:

'In all the forms of marriage given in this chapter of this work, the one that precedes is better than the one that follows it on account of its being more in accordance with the commands of religion, and therefore it is only when it is impossible to carry the former into practice that the latter should be resorted to. As the fruit of all good marriages is love, the Gandharva form of marriage is respected, even though it is formed under unfavourable circumstances, because it fulfils the object sought for. Another cause of the respect accorded to the Gandharva form of marriage is that it brings forth happiness, causes less trouble in its performance than the other forms of marriage, and is above all the result of previous love.'

1 These forms of marriage differ from the four kinds of marriage mentioned in Chapter 1, and are only to be made use of when the girl is gained over in the way mentioned in Chapters 3 and 4.

2 A marriage contracted by mutual consent between two lovers, without the consent of their parents and without formal rituals. This form of marriage is said to have been based on the customs of the Gandharvas, an ancient tribe mentioned in the *Mahabharata*. (ed.)

PART FOUR

ABOUT A WIFE

CHAPTER 1

ON THE MANNER OF LIVING
OF A VIRTUOUS WOMAN

A VIRTUOUS WOMAN, WHO HAS AFFECTION for her husband, should act in conformity with his wishes as if he were a divine being, and with his consent should take upon herself the whole care of his family. She should keep the whole house well cleaned, and arrange flowers of various kinds in different parts of it, and make the floor smooth and polished so as to give the whole a neat and becoming appearance. She should surround the house with a garden, and place ready in it all the materials required for the morning, noon and evening sacrifices. Moreover she should herself revere the sanctuary of the Household Gods, for, says Gonardiya, 'nothing so much attracts the heart of a householder to his wife as a careful observance of the things mentioned above'.

Towards the parents, relations, friends, sisters, and servants of her husband she should behave as they deserve. In the garden she should plant beds of green vegetables, bunches of the sugar cane, and clumps of the fig tree. Clusters of various flowers such as the jasmine, the yellow amaranth, the wild jasmine, the China rose and others, should likewise be planted, together with the fragrant grass *Andropogon schaenanthus*, and the fragrant root of the plant *Andropogon miricatus*. She should also have seats and arbours made in the garden, in the middle of which a well, tank, or pool should be dug.

The wife should always avoid the company of female beggars, female Buddhist mendicants, unchaste and roguish women, female fortune tellers and witches. As regards meals she should always consider what her husband likes and dislikes and what things are good for him, and what are injurious to him. When she hears the sounds of his footsteps coming home she should at once get up and be ready to do whatever he may command her, and either order her female servant to wash his feet, or wash them herself. When going anywhere with her husband, she should put on her ornaments, and without his consent she should not either give or accept invitations, or attend marriages and sacrifices, or sit in the company of female friends, or visit the temples of the Gods. And if she wants to engage in any kind of games or sports, she should not do it against his will. In the same way she should always sit down after him, and get up before him, and should never awaken him when he is asleep. The kitchen should be situated in a quiet and retired place, so as not to be accessible to strangers, and should always look clean.

In the event of any misconduct on the part of her husband, she should not blame him excessively, though she be a little displeased. She should not use abusive language towards him, but rebuke him with conciliatory words, whether he be in the company of friends or alone. Moreover, she should not be a scold, for, says Gonardiya, 'there is no cause of dislike on the part of a husband so great as this characteristic in a wife'. Lastly she should avoid bad expressions, sulky looks, speaking aside, standing in the doorway, and looking at passers-by, conversing in the pleasure groves, and remaining in a lonely place for a long time; and finally she should always keep her body, her teeth, her hair and everything belonging to her tidy, sweet, and clean.

When the wife wants to approach her husband in private her dress should consist of many ornaments, various kinds of flowers, and a cloth decorated with different colours, and some sweet-smelling ointments or unguents. But her everyday dress should be composed of a thin, close-textured cloth, a few ornaments and flowers, and a little scent, not too much. She should also observe the fasts and vows of her husband, and when he tries to prevent her doing this, she should persuade him to let her do it.

At appropriate times of the year, and when they happen to be cheap, she should buy earth, bamboos, firewood, skins, and iron pots, as also salt and oil. Fragrant substances, and other things which are always wanted, should be obtained when required and kept in a secret place of the house. The seeds of vegetables should be bought and sown at the proper seasons. The wife, moreover, should not tell to strangers the amount of her wealth, nor the secrets which her husband has confided to her. She should surpass all the women of her own rank in life in her cleverness, her appearance, her knowledge of cookery, her pride, and her manner of serving her husband. The expenditure of the year should be regulated by the profits. The milk that remains after the meals should be turned into ghee or clarified butter. Oil and sugar should be prepared

at home; spinning and weaving should also be done there; and a store of ropes and cords, and barks of trees for twisting into ropes should be kept. She should also attend to the pounding and cleaning of rice, using its small grain and chaff in some way or other. She should pay the salaries of the servants, look after the tilling of the fields, and keeping of the flocks and herds, superintend the making of vehicles, and take care of the rams, cocks, quails, parrots, starlings, cuckoos, peacocks, monkeys, and deer; and finally adjust the income and expenditure of the day. The worn-out clothes should be given to those servants who have done good work, in order to show them that their services have been appreciated, or they may be applied to some other use. The vessels in which wine is prepared, as well as those in which it is kept, should be carefully looked after, and put away at the proper time. All sales and purchases should also be well attended to. The friends of her husband she should welcome by presenting them with flowers, ointment, incense, betel leaves, and betel nut. Her father-in-law and mother-in-law she should treat as they deserve, always remaining dependent on their will, never contradicting them, speaking to them in few and not harsh words, not laughing loudly in their presence, and acting with their friends and enemies as with her own. In addition to the above she should not be vain, or too much taken up with her enjoyments. She should be liberal towards her servants, and reward them on holidays and festivals; and not give away anything without first making it known to her husband.

Thus ends the manner of living of a virtuous woman.

There are also some verses on the subject as follows:

'The wife, whether she be a woman of noble family, or a virgin widow[1] remarried, or a concubine, should lead a chaste life, devoted to her husband, and doing everything for his welfare. Women acting thus acquire Dharma, Artha, *and* Kama, *obtain a high position, and generally keep their husbands devoted to them.'*

1 This probably refers to a girl married in her infancy, or when very young and whose husband had died before she arrived at the age of puberty. Infant marriages are still the common custom of the Hindus.

ON THE CONDUCT OF THE ELDEST WIFE TOWARDS THE OTHER WIVES OF HER HUSBAND, AND ON THAT OF A YOUNGER WIFE TOWARDS THE ELDER ONES. ALSO ON THE CONDUCT OF A WIFE DISLIKED BY HER HUSBAND, AND ON THE CONDUCT OF A HUSBAND TOWARDS MANY WIVES

THE CAUSES OF RE-MARRYING during the lifetime of the wife are
as follows:

- The folly or ill-temper of the wife
- Her husband's dislike to her
- The want of offspring
- The continual birth of daughters
- The incontinence of the husband.

From the very beginning, a wife should endeavour to attract the heart
of her husband, by showing to him continually her devotion, her good
temper, and her wisdom. If, however, she bears him no children, she
should herself tell her husband to marry another woman. And when the
second wife is married, and brought to the house, the first wife should
give her a position superior to her own, and look upon her as a sister. In
the morning the elder wife should forcibly make the younger one decorate
herself in the presence of their husband, and should not mind all the
husband's favour being given to her. If the younger wife does anything to
displease her husband the elder one should not neglect her, but should
always be ready to give her most careful advice, and should teach her to
do various things in the presence of her husband. Her children she should
treat as her own, her attendants she should look upon with more regard
even than on her own servants, her friends she should cherish with love
and kindness, and her relations with great honour.

When there are many other wives besides herself, the elder wife
should associate with the one who is immediately next to her in rank
and age, and should instigate the wife who has recently enjoyed her
husband's favour to quarrel with the present favourite. After this she
should sympathize with the former, and having collected all the other
wives together, should get them to denounce the favourite as a scheming
and wicked woman, without however committing herself in any way. If
the favourite wife happens to quarrel with the husband, then the elder
wife should take her part and give her false encouragement, and thus
cause the quarrel to be increased. If there be only a little quarrel between
the two, the elder wife should do all she can to work it up into a large
quarrel. But if after all this she finds the husband still continues to love
his favourite wife she should then change her tactics, and endeavour to
bring about a conciliation between them, so as to avoid her husband's
displeasure.

Thus ends the conduct of the elder wife.

THE YOUNGER WIFE should regard the elder wife of her husband as
her mother, and should not give anything away, even to her own relations,

without her knowledge. She should tell her everything about herself, and not approach her husband without her permission. Whatever is told to her by the elder wife she should not reveal to others, and she should take care of the children of the senior even more than of her own. When alone with her husband she should serve him well, but should not tell him of the pain she suffers from the existence of a rival wife. She may also obtain secretly from her husband some marks of his particular regard for her, and may tell him that she lives only for him, and for the regard that he has for her. She should never reveal her love for her husband, nor her husband's love for her to any person, either in pride or in anger, for a wife that reveals the secrets of her husband is despised by him. As for seeking to obtain the regard of her husband, Gonardiya says, that it should always be done in private, for fear of the elder wife.

Thus ends the conduct of the younger wife towards the elder.

A WOMAN WHO IS DISLIKED BY HER HUSBAND, and annoyed and distressed by his other wives, should associate with the wife who is liked most by her husband, and who serves him more than the others, and should teach her all the arts with which she is acquainted. She should act as the nurse to her husband's children, and having gained over his friends to her side, should through them make him acquainted of her devotion to him. In religious ceremonies she should be a leader, as also in vows and fasts, and should not hold too good an opinion of herself. When her husband is lying on his bed she should only go near him when it is agreeable to him, and should never rebuke him, or show obstinacy in any way. If her husband happens to quarrel with any of his other wives, she should reconcile them to each other, and if he desires to see any woman secretly, she should manage to bring about the meeting between them. She should moreover make herself acquainted with the weak points of her husband's character, but always keep them secret, and on the whole behave herself in such a way as may lead him to look upon her as a good and devoted wife.

Here ends the conduct of a wife disliked by her husband.

A MAN MARRYING MANY WIVES should act fairly towards them all. He should neither disregard nor pass over their faults, and should not reveal to one wife the love, passion, bodily blemishes and confidential reproaches of the other. No opportunity should be given to any one of them of speaking to him about their rivals, and if one of them should begin to speak ill of another, he should chide her and tell her that she has exactly the same blemishes in her character. One of them he should please by secret confidence, another by secret respect, and another by secret flattery, and he should please them all by going to gardens, by amusements, by presents, by honouring their relations, by telling them secrets, and lastly by loving unions. A young woman who is of a good temper, and who conducts herself according to the precepts of the Holy Writ, wins her husband's attachments, and obtains a superiority over her rivals.

Thus ends the conduct of a husband towards many wives.

PART FIVE

ABOUT THE WIVES OF OTHER MEN

ON THE CHARACTERISTICS OF MEN AND WOMEN, AND THE REASONS WHY WOMEN REJECT THE ADDRESSES OF MEN

THE WIVES OF OTHER PEOPLE may be resorted to on the occasions already described in Part One, Chapter 5 of this work, but the possibility of their acquisition, their fitness for cohabitation, the danger to oneself in uniting with them, and the future effect of these unions, should first of all be examined. A man may resort to the wife of another, for the purpose of saving his own life, when he perceives that his love for her proceeds from one degree of intensity to another. These degrees are ten in number, and are distinguished by the following marks:

- Love of the eye
- Attachment of the mind
- Constant reflection
- Destruction of sleep
- Emaciation of the body
- Turning away from objects of enjoyment
- Removal of shame
- Madness
- Fainting
- Death.

Ancient authors say that a man should know the disposition, truthfulness, purity, and will of a young woman, as also the intensity, or weakness of her passions, from the form of her body, and from her characteristic marks and signs. But Vatsyayana is of opinion that the forms of bodies and the characteristic marks or signs are but erring tests of character, and that women should be judged by their conduct, by the outward expression of their thoughts, and by the movements of their bodies.

Now as a general rule Gonikaputra says that a woman falls in love with every handsome man she sees, and so does every man at the sight of a beautiful woman, but frequently they do not take any further steps, owing to various considerations. In love, the following circumstances are peculiar to the woman. She loves without regard to right or wrong, and does not try to gain over a man simply for the attainment of some particular purpose. Moreover, when a man first makes up to her she naturally shrinks from him, even though she may be willing to unite herself with him. But when the attempts to gain her are repeated and renewed, she at last consents. But with a man, even though he may have begun to love, he conquers his feelings from a regard for morality and wisdom, and although his thoughts are often on the woman, he does not yield, even though an attempt be made to gain him over. He sometimes makes an attempt or effort to win the object of his affections, and having failed, he leaves her alone for the future. In the same way, when a woman is once gained, he often becomes indifferent about her. As for the saying that a man does not care for what is easily gained, and only desires a thing which cannot be obtained without difficulty, it is only a matter of talk.

The causes of a woman rejecting the addresses of a man are as follows:

- Affection for her husband
- Desire of lawful progeny
- Want of opportunity
- Anger at being addressed by the man too familiarly
- Difference in rank of life
- Want of certainty on account of the man being devoted to travelling
- Thinking that the man may be attached to some other person
- Fear of the man's not keeping his intentions secret
- Distrust of his low character
- Fear of discovery
- Fear that he may be employed by her husband to test her chastity.

Whichever of the above causes a man may detect, he should endeavour to remove it from the very beginning.

There are also some verses on the subject as follows:

'Desire, which springs from nature, and which is increased by art, and from which all danger is taken away by wisdom, becomes firm and secure. A clever man, depending on his own ability, and observing carefully the ideas and thoughts of women, and removing the causes of their turning away from men, is generally successful with them.'

126

CHAPTER 2

ABOUT MAKING ACQUAINTANCE WITH THE WOMAN, AND OF THE EFFORTS TO GAIN HER OVER

ANCIENT AUTHORS ARE OF OPINION that girls are not so easily seduced by employing female messengers as by the efforts of the man himself, but that the wives of others are more easily got at by the aid of female messengers than by the personal efforts of the man. But Vatsyayana lays it down that whenever it is possible a man should always act himself in these matters, and it is only when such is impracticable, or impossible, that female messengers should be employed. As for the saying that women who act and talk boldly and freely are to be won by the personal efforts of the man, and that women who do not possess those qualities are to be got at by female messengers, it is only a matter of talk.

Now when a man acts himself in the matter he should first of all make the acquaintance of the woman he loves in the following manner:

He should arrange to be seen by the woman either on a natural or special opportunity. A natural opportunity is when one of them goes to the house of the other, and a special opportunity is when they meet either at the house of a friend, or a caste-fellow, or a minister, or a physician, as also on the occasion of marriage ceremonies, sacrifices, festivals, funerals, and garden parties.

When they do meet, the man should be careful to look at her in such a way as to cause the state of his mind to be made known to her: he should pull about his moustache, make a sound with his nails, cause his own ornaments to tinkle, bite his lower lip, and make various other signs of that description. When she is looking at him he should speak to his friends about her and other women, and should show to her his liberality and his appreciation of enjoyments. When sitting by the side of a female friend he should yawn and twist his body, contract his eyebrows, speak very slowly as if he was weary, and listen to her indifferently. A conversation having two meanings should also be carried on with a child or some other person, apparently having regard to a third person, but really having reference to the woman he loves, and in this way his love should be made manifest under the pretext of referring to others rather than to herself. All these things should be done at the proper time and in proper places.

The man should fondle a child that may be sitting on her lap, and give it something to play with, and also take the same back again. Conversation with respect to the child may also be held with her, and in this manner he should gradually become well acquainted with her, and he should also make himself agreeable to her relations. Afterwards, this acquaintance should be made a pretext for visiting her house frequently, and on such occasions he should converse on the subject of love in her absence but within her hearing. As his intimacy with her increases he should place in her charge some kind of deposit or trust, and take away from it a small portion at a time; or he may give her some fragrant substances, or betel nuts to be kept for him by her. After this he should endeavour to make her well acquainted with his own wife, and get them to carry on confidential conversations, and to sit together in lonely places. In order to see her frequently he should arrange so that the same goldsmith, the same jeweller, the same basket maker, the same dyer, and the same washerman should be employed by the two families. And he should also pay her long visits openly under the pretence of being engaged with her on business, and one business should lead to another, so as to keep up the intercourse between them. Whenever she wants anything, or is in need of money, or wishes to acquire skill in one of the arts, he should cause her to understand that he is willing and able to do anything that she wants, to give her money, or teach her one of the arts, all these things being quite within his ability and power. In the same way he should hold discussions with her in company with other people, and they should talk of the doings and sayings of other persons, and examine different things, like jewellery, precious stones, etc. On such occasions he should show her certain things with the values of which she may be unacquainted, and if she begins to dispute with him about the things or their value, he should not contradict her, but point out that he agrees with her in every way.

Thus end the ways of making the acquaintance of woman desired.

When a man is endeavouring to seduce one woman, he should not attempt to seduce any other at the same time. But after he has succeeded with the first, and enjoyed her for a considerable time, he can keep her affections by giving her presents that she likes, and then commence making up to another woman. When a man sees the husband of a woman going to some place near his house, he should not enjoy the woman then, even though she may be easily gained over at that time. A wise man having a regard for his reputation should not think of seducing a woman who is apprehensive, timid, not to be trusted, well guarded, or possessed of a father-in-law, or mother-in-law.

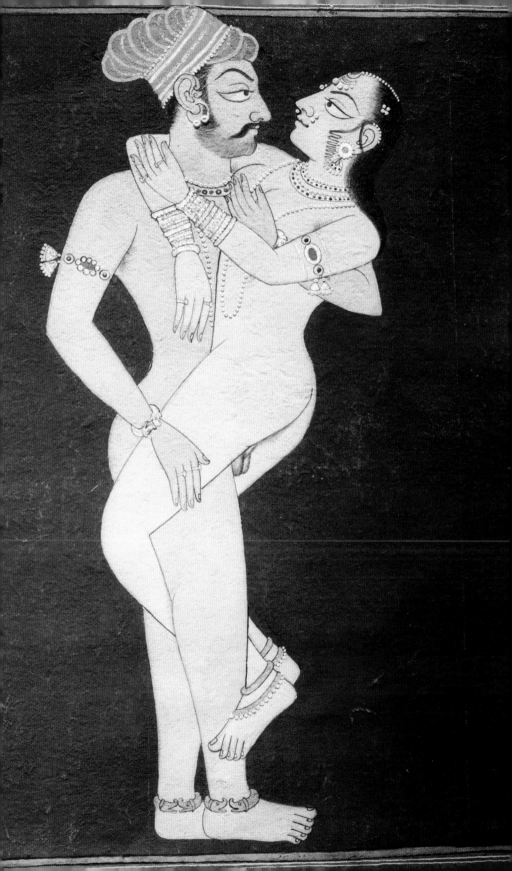

CHAPTER 3

Examination of the State of a Woman's Mind

WHEN A MAN IS TRYING TO GAIN over a woman he should examine the state of her mind, and act as follows:

If she listens to him, but does not manifest to him in any way her own intentions, he should then try to gain her over by means of a go-between.

If she meets him once, and again comes to meet him better dressed than before, or comes to him in some lonely place, he should be certain that she is capable of being enjoyed by the use of a little force.

A woman who lets a man make up to her, but does not give herself up, even after a long time, should be considered as a trifler in love, but owing to the fickleness of the human mind, even such a woman can be conquered by always keeping up a close acquaintance with her.

When a woman avoids the attentions of a man, and on account of respect for him, and pride in herself, will not meet him or approach him, she can be gained over with difficulty, either by endeavouring to keep on familiar terms with her, or else by an exceedingly clever go-between.

When a man makes up to a woman, and she reproaches him with harsh words, she should be abandoned at once.

When a woman reproaches a man, but at the same time acts affectionately towards him, she should be made love to in every way.

A woman, who meets a man in lonely places, and puts up with the touch of his foot, but pretends, on account of the indecision of her mind, not to be aware of it, should be conquered by patience, and by continued efforts as follows:

If she happens to go to sleep in his vicinity he should put his left arm round her, and see when she awakes whether she repulses him in reality,

or only repulses him in such a way as if she was desirous of the same thing being done to her again. And what is done by the arm can also be done by the foot. If the man succeeds in this point he should embrace her more closely, and if she will not stand the embrace and gets up, but behaves with him as usual the next day, he should consider then that she is not unwilling to be enjoyed by him.

When a woman neither gives encouragement to a man, nor avoids him, but hides herself and remains in some lonely place, she must be got at by means of the female servant who may be near her. If when called by the man she acts in the same way, then she should be gained over by means of a skilful go-between. But if she will have nothing to say to the man, he should consider well about her before he begins any further attempts to gain her over.

Thus ends the examination of the state of a woman's mind.

A man should first get himself introduced to a woman, and then carry on a conversation with her. He should give her hints of his love for her, and if he finds from her replies that she receives these hints favourably, he should then set to work to gain her over without any fear. A woman who shows her love by outward signs to the man at his first interview should be gained over very easily. In the same way a lascivious woman, who when addressed in loving words replies openly in words expressive of her love, should be considered to have been gained over at that very moment. With regard to all women, whether they be wise, simple, or confiding, this rule is laid down that those who make an open manifestation of their love are easily gained over.

134

CHAPTER 4

ABOUT THE BUSINESS
OF A GO-BETWEEN

IF A WOMAN HAS MANIFESTED HER LOVE or desire, either by signs or by motions of the body, and is afterwards rarely or never seen anywhere, or if a woman is met for the first time, the man should get a go-between to approach her.

Now the go-between, having wheedled herself into the confidence of the woman by acting according to her disposition, should try to make her hate or despise her husband by holding artful conversations with her, by telling her about medicines for getting children, by talking to her about other people, by tales of various kinds, by stories about the wives of other men, and by praising her beauty, wisdom, generosity and good nature, and then saying to her: 'It is indeed a pity that you, who are so excellent a woman in every way, should be possessed of a husband of this kind. Beautiful lady, he is not fit even to serve you.' The go-between should further talk to the woman about the weakness of the passion of her husband, his jealousy, his roguery, his ingratitude, his aversion to enjoyments, his dullness, his meanness, and all the other faults that he may have, and with which she may be acquainted. She should particularly harp upon that fault or that failing by which the wife may appear to be the most affected. If the wife be a deer woman, and the husband a hare man, then there would be no fault in that direction, but in the event of his being a hare man, and she a mare woman or elephant woman, then this fault should be pointed out to her.

Gonikaputra is of the opinion that when it is the first affair of the woman, or when her love has only been very secretly shown, the man should then secure and send to her a go-between, with whom she may be already acquainted, and in whom she confides.

But to return to our subject. The go-between should tell the woman about the obedience and love of the man, and as her confidence and affection increase, she should then explain to her the thing to be accomplished in the following way. 'Hear this, O beautiful lady, that this man, born of a good family, having seen you, has gone mad on your account. The poor young man, who is tender by nature, has never been distressed in such a way before, and it is highly probable that he will succumb under his present affliction, and experience the pains of death.' If the woman listens with a favourable ear, then on the following day the go-between, having observed marks of good spirits in her face, in her eyes, and in her manner of conversation, should again converse with her on the subject of the man, and should tell her the stories of Ahalya[1] and Indra, of Sakoontala[2] and Dushyanti, and such others as may be fitted for the occasion. She should also describe to her the strength of the man, his talents, his skill in the sixty-four sorts of enjoyments mentioned by Babhravya, his good looks, and his liaison with some praiseworthy woman, no matter whether this last ever took place or not.

In addition to this, the go-between should carefully note the behaviour of the woman, which if favourable would be as follows: she would address her with a smiling look, would seat herself close beside her, and ask her, 'Where have you been? What have you been doing? Where did you dine? Where did you sleep? Where have you been sitting?' Moreover, the woman would meet the go-between in lonely places and tell her stories there, would yawn contemplatively, draw long sighs, give her presents, remember her on occasions of festivals, dismiss her with a wish to see her again, and say to her jestingly, 'Oh, well-speaking woman, why do you speak these bad words to me?', would discourse on the sin of her union with the man, would not tell her about any previous visits or conversations that she may have had with him, but wish to be asked about these, and lastly would laugh at the man's desire, but would not reproach him in any way.

Thus ends the behaviour of the woman with the go-between.

Now go-betweens or female messengers are of the following different kinds:

- A go-between who takes upon herself the whole burden of the business
- A go-between who does only a limited part of the business
- A go-between who is the bearer of a letter only
- A go-between acting on her own account.

A woman who, having observed the mutual passion of a man and woman, brings them together and arranges it by the power of her own intellect, such a one is called a go-between who takes upon herself the whole burden of the business. This kind of go-between is chiefly employed when the man and the woman are already acquainted with each other, and have conversed together, and in such cases she is sent not only by the man (as is always done in all other cases) but by the woman also. The above name is also given to a go-between who, perceiving that the man and the woman are suited to each other, tries to bring about a union between them, even though they be not acquainted with each other.

A go-between who, perceiving that some part of the affair is already done, or that the advances on the part of the man are already made, completes the rest of the business, is called a go-between who performs only a limited part of the business.

A go-between who simply carries messages between a man and a woman, who love each other, but who cannot frequently meet, is called the bearer of a letter or message.

This name is also given to one who is sent by either of the lovers to acquaint either the one or the other with the time and place of their meeting.

A woman who goes herself to a man, and tells him of her having enjoyed sexual union with him in a dream, and expresses her anger at his wife having rebuked him for calling her by the name of her rival instead of by her own name, and gives him something bearing the marks of her teeth and nails and informs him that she knew she was formerly desired by him, and asks him privately whether she or his wife is the best looking, such a person is called a woman who is a go-between for herself. Now such a woman should be met and interviewed by the man in private and secretly.

The above name is also given to a woman who having made an agreement with some other woman to act as her go-between, gains over the man to herself, by the means of making him personally acquainted with herself, and thus causes the other woman to fail. The same applies to a man who, acting as a go-between for another, and having no previous connection with the woman, gains her over for himself, and thus causes the failure of the other man.

Thus end the different kinds of go-betweens.

A female astrologer, a female servant, a female beggar, or a female artist are well acquainted with the business of a go-between, and very soon gain the confidence of other women. Any one of them can raise enmity between any two persons if she wishes to do so, or extol the loveliness of any woman that she wishes to praise, or describe the arts practised by other women in sexual union. They can also speak highly of the love of a man, of his skill in sexual enjoyment, and of the desire of other women, more beautiful even than the woman they are addressing, for him, and explain the restraint under which he may be at home.

Lastly a go-between can, by the artfulness of her conversation, unite a woman with a man even though he may not have been thought of by her, or may have been considered beyond her aspirations. She can also bring back a man to a woman, who, owing to some cause or other, has separated himself from her.

1 The wife of the sage Gautama, she was seduced by Indra, the king of the Gods.

2 The heroine of one of the best, if not the best, of Hindu plays, and the best known in Sanskrit dramatic literature.

ABOUT THE LOVE OF PERSONS IN AUTHORITY FOR THE WIVES OF OTHER MEN

KINGS AND THEIR MINISTERS have no access to the abodes of others, and moreover their mode of living is constantly watched and observed and imitated by the people at large, just as the animal world, seeing the sun rise, get up after him, and when he sits in the evening, lie down again in the same way. Persons in authority should not therefore do any improper act in public, as such are impossible from their position, and would be deserving of censure. But if they find that such an act is necessary to be done, they should make use of the proper means as described in the following paragraphs.

The head man of the village, the king's officer employed there, and the man[1] whose business it is to glean corn, can gain over female villagers simply by asking them. It is on this account that this class of woman are called unchaste women by voluptuaries.

The union of the above mentioned men with this class of woman takes place on the occasions of unpaid labour, of filling the granaries in their houses, of taking things in and out of the house, of cleaning the houses, of working in the fields, and of purchasing cotton, wool, flax, hemp, and thread, and at the season of the purchase, sale, and exchange of various other articles, as well as at the time of doing various other works. In the same way the superintendents of cow pens enjoy the women in the cow pens; and the officers, who crave the superintendence of widows, of the women who are without supporters, and of women who have left their husbands, have sexual

intercourse with these women. The intelligent accomplish their object by wandering at night in the village, and while villagers also unite with the wives of their sons, being much alone with them. Lastly the superintendents of markets have a great deal to do with the female villagers at the time of their making purchases in the market.

During the festival of the eighth moon, i.e. during the bright half of the month of Nargashirsha, as also during the moonlight festival of the month of Kartika, and the spring festival of Chaitra, the women of cities and towns generally visit the women of the king's harem in the royal palace. These visitors go to the several apartments of the women of the harem, as they are acquainted with them, and pass the night in conversation, and in proper sports, and amusement, and go away in the morning. On such occasions a female attendant of the king (previously acquainted with the woman whom the king desires) should loiter about, and accost this woman when she sets out to go home, and induce her to come and see the amusing things in the palace. Previous to these festivals even, she should have caused it to be intimated to this woman that on the occasion of this festival she would show her all the interesting things in the royal palace. Accordingly she should show her the bower of the coral creeper, the garden house with its floor inlaid with precious stones, the bower of grapes, the building on the water, the secret passages in the walls of the palace, the pictures, the sporting animals, the machines, the birds, and the cages of the lions and the tigers. After this, when alone with her, she should tell her about the love of the king for her, and should describe to her the good fortune which would attend upon her union with the king, giving her at the time a strict promise of secrecy. If the woman does not accept the offer, she should conciliate and please her with handsome presents befitting the position of the king, and having accompanied her for some distance should dismiss her with great affection.

Or, having made the acquaintance of the husband of the woman whom the king desires, the wives of the king should get the wife to pay them a visit in the harem, and on this occasion a female attendant of the king, having been sent thither, should act as above described.

Or, one of the king's wives should get acquainted with the woman that the king desires, by sending one of the female attendants to her, who should, on their becoming more intimate, induce her to come and see the royal abode. Afterwards when she has visited the harem, and acquired confidence, a female confidante of the king, sent thither, should act as before described.

Or, the king's wife should invite the woman, whom the king desires, to come to the royal palace, so that she might see the practice of the art in which the king's wife may be skilled, and after she has come to the harem, a female attendant of the king, sent thither, should act as before described.

Lastly, if the woman desired by the king be living with some person who is not her husband, then the king should cause her to be arrested, and having made her a slave, on account of her crime, should place her in the harem. Or the king should cause his ambassador to quarrel with the husband of the woman desired by him, and should then imprison her as the wife of an enemy of the king, and by this means should place her in the harem.

Thus end the means of gaining over the wives of others secretly.

There are also two verses on the subject as follows:

'The above and other ways are the means employed in different countries by kings with regard to the wives of other persons. But a king, who has the welfare of his people at heart, should not on any account put them into practice.'

'A king, who has conquered the six[2] enemies of mankind, becomes the master of the whole earth.'

1 This is a phrase used for a man who does the work of everybody, and who is fed by the whole village.

2 These are Lust, Anger, Avarice, Spiritual Ignorance, Pride, and Envy.

CHAPTER 6

About the women of the royal harem, and of the keeping of one's own wife

THE WOMEN OF THE ROYAL HAREM cannot see or meet any men on account of their being strictly guarded, neither do they have their desires satisfied, because their only husband is common to many wives. For this reason among themselves they give pleasure to each other in various ways as now described.

Having dressed the daughters of their nurses, or their female friends, or their female attendants, like men, they accomplish their object by means of bulbs, roots, and fruits having the form of the *lingam*, or they lie down upon the statue of a male figure, in which the *lingam* is visible and erect.

Some kings, who are compassionate, take or apply certain medicines to enable them to enjoy many wives in one night, simply for the purpose of satisfying the desire of their women, though they perhaps have no desire of their own. Others enjoy with great affection only those wives that they particularly like, while others only take them, according as the turn of each wife arrives in due course. Such are the ways of enjoyment prevalent in Eastern countries, and what is said about the means of enjoyment of the female is also applicable to the male.

By means of their female attendants the ladies of the royal harem generally get men into their apartments in the disguise or dress of women. Their female attendants, and the daughters of their nurses, who are acquainted with their secrets, should exert themselves to get men to come to the harem in this way by telling them of the good fortune attending it, and by describing the facilities of entering and leaving the palace, the large size of the premises, the carelessness of the sentinels, and the irregularities of the attendants about the persons of the royal wives. But these women should never induce a man to enter the harem by telling him falsehoods, for that would probably lead to his destruction.

As for the man himself he had better not enter a royal harem, even though it may be easily accessible, on account of the numerous disasters to which he may be exposed there. If however he wants to enter it, he should first ascertain whether there is an easy way to get out, whether it is closely surrounded by the pleasure garden, whether it has separate enclosures belonging to it, whether the sentinels are careless, whether the king has gone abroad, and then, when he is called by the women of the harem, he should carefully observe the localities, and enter by the way pointed out by them. If he is able to manage it, he should hang about the harem every day, and under some pretext or other, make friends with the sentinels, and show himself attached to the female attendants of the harem, who may have become acquainted with his design, and to whom he should express his regret at not being able to obtain the object of his desire. Lastly he should cause the whole business of a go-between to be done by the woman who may have access to the harem, and he should be careful to be able to recognize the emissaries of the king.

When a go-between has no access to the harem, then the man should stand in some place where the lady, whom he loves and whom he is anxious to enjoy, can be seen.

If that place is occupied by the king's sentinels, he should then disguise himself as a female attendant of the lady who comes to the place, or passes by it. When she looks at him he should let her know his feelings by outward signs and gestures, and should show her pictures, things with double meanings, chaplets of flowers, and rings. He should carefully mark the answer she gives, whether by word or by sign, or by gesture, and should then try and get into the harem. If he is certain of her coming to some particular place he should conceal himself there, and at the appointed time should enter along with her as one of the guards.

The entrance of young men into harems, and their exit from them, generally take place when things are being brought into the palace, or when things are being taken out of it, or when drinking festivals are going on, or when the female attendants are in a hurry, or when the residence of some of the royal ladies is being changed, or when the king's wives go to gardens,

148

or to fairs, or when they enter the palace on their return from them, or lastly, when the king is absent on a long pilgrimage. The women of the royal harem know each other's secrets, and having but one object to attain, they give assistance to each other. A young man, who enjoys all of them, and who is common to them all, can continue enjoying his union with them so long as it is kept quiet, and is not known abroad.

Thus act the wives of others.

For these reasons a man should guard his own wife. Vatsyayana says that, as wicked persons are always successful with women, a man should not cause his innocent wife to be corrupted by bringing her into the company of a deceitful woman.

The following are the causes of the destruction of a woman's chastity:

- Always going into society, and sitting in company
- Absence of restraint
- The loose habits of her husband
- Want of caution in her relations with other men
- Continued and long absence of her husband
- Living in a foreign country
- Destruction of her love and feelings by her husband
- The company of loose women
- The jealousy of her husband.

There are also the following verses on the subject:

'A clever man, learning from the Shastras *the ways of winning over the wives of other people, is never deceived in the case of his own wives. No one, however, should make use of these ways for seducing the wives of others, because they do not always succeed, and, moreover, often cause disasters, and the destruction of* Dharma *and* Artha. *This book, which is intended for the good of the people, and to teach them the ways of guarding their own wives, should not be made use of merely for gaining over the wives of others.'*

PART SIX

ABOUT
COURTESANS

ON THE CAUSES OF A COURTESAN RESORTING TO MEN, AND OF THE MEANS OF ATTACHING TO HERSELF THE MAN DESIRED

BY HAVING INTERCOURSE WITH MEN courtesans obtain sexual pleasure, as well as their own maintenance. Now when a courtesan takes up with a man from love, the action is natural; but when she resorts to him for the purpose of getting money, her action is artificial or forced. Even in the latter case, however, she should conduct herself as if her love were indeed natural, because men repose their confidence on those women who apparently love them. In making known her love to the man, she should show an entire freedom from avarice, and for the sake of her future credit she should abstain from acquiring money from him by unlawful means.

A courtesan, well dressed and wearing her ornaments, should sit or stand at the door of her house, and, without exposing herself too much, should look on the public road so as to be seen by the passers by, she being like an object on view for sale. She should form friendships with such persons as would enable her to separate men from other women, and attach them to herself, to repair her own misfortunes, to acquire wealth, and to protect her from being bullied or set upon by persons with whom she may have dealings of some kind or another.

The woman also should have the following characteristics:

She should be possessed of beauty, and amiability, with auspicious body marks. She should have a liking for good qualities in other people, as also a liking for wealth.

She should take delight in sexual unions, resulting from love, and should be of a firm mind, and of the same class as the man with regard to sexual enjoyment.

She should always be anxious to acquire and obtain experience and knowledge, be free from avarice, and always have a liking for social gatherings, and for the arts.

The following are the ordinary qualities of all women:

To be possessed of intelligence, good disposition, and good manners; to be straightforward in behaviour, and to be grateful; to consider well the future before doing anything; to possess activity, to be of consistent behaviour, and to have a knowledge of the proper times and places for doing things; to speak always without meanness, loud laughter, malignity, anger, avarice, dullness, or stupidity; to have a knowledge of the *Kama Sutra*, and to be skilled in all the arts connected with it.

The faults of women are to be known by the absence of any of the above-mentioned good qualities.

Ancient authors are of opinion that the causes of a courtesan resorting to men are love, fear, money, pleasure, returning some act of enmity, curiosity, sorrow, constant intercourse, *Dharma*, celebrity, compassion, the desire of having a friend, shame, the likeness of the man to some beloved person, the search after good fortune, the getting rid of the love of somebody else, the being of the same class as the man with respect to sexual union, living in the same place, constancy, and poverty. But Vatsyayana decides that desire of wealth, freedom from misfortune, and love are the only causes that affect the union of courtesans with men.

Now a courtesan should not sacrifice money to her love, because money is the chief thing to be attended to. But in cases of fear, etc., she should pay regard to strength and other qualities. Moreover, even though she be invited by any man to join him, she should not at once consent to a union, because men are apt to despise things which are easily acquired. On such occasions she should first ascertain whether the man is pure or impure, affected, or the reverse, capable of attachment, or indifferent, liberal or niggardly; and if she finds him to her liking, she should then employ the *Vita* and others to attach his mind to her.

Accordingly, the *Pithamarda* should bring the man to her house, under the pretence of seeing the fights of quails, cocks, and rams, of hearing the mania (a kind of starling) talk, or of seeing some other spectacle, or the practice of some art; or he may take the woman to the abode of the man. After this, when the man comes to her house the woman should give him something capable of producing curiosity, and love in his heart, such as an affectionate present, telling him that it was specially designed

for his use. She should also amuse him for a long time by telling him such stories, and doing such things as he may take most delight in. When he goes away she should frequently send to him a female attendant, skilled in carrying on a jesting conversation, and also a small present at the same time. She should also sometimes go to him herself under the pretence of some business, and accompanied by the *Pithamarda*.

Thus end the means of attaching to herself the man desired.

There are also some verses on the subject as follows:

> '*When a lover comes to her abode, a courtesan should give him a mixture of betel leaves and betel nut, garlands of flowers, and perfumed ointments, and, showing her skill in arts, should entertain him with a long conversation. She should also give him some loving presents, and make an exchange of her own things with his, and at the same time should show him her skill in sexual enjoyment. When a courtesan is thus united with her lover she should always delight him by affectionate gifts, by conversation, and by the application of tender means of enjoyment.*'

CHAPTER 2

ON A COURTESAN LIVING LIKE A WIFE

WHEN A COURTESAN IS LIVING AS A WIFE with her lover, she should behave like a chaste woman, and do everything to his satisfaction. Her duty in this respect, in short, is, that she should give him pleasure, but should not become attached to him, though behaving as if she were really attached.

Now the following is the manner in which she is to conduct herself, so as to accomplish the above-mentioned purpose. She should have a mother dependent on her, one who should be represented as very harsh, and who looked upon money as her chief object in life. In the event of there being no mother, then an old and confidential nurse should play the same role. The mother or nurse, on their part, should appear to be displeased with the lover, and forcibly take her away from him. The woman herself should always show pretended anger, dejection, fear, and shame on this account, but should not disobey the mother or nurse at any time.

She should make out to the mother or nurse that the man is suffering from bad health, and making this a pretext for going to see him, she should go on that account. She is, moreover, to do the following things for the purpose of gaining the man's favour:

Sending her female attendant to bring the flowers used by him on the previous day, in order that she may use them herself as a mark of affection, also asking for the mixture of betel nut and leaves that have remained uneaten by him; expressing wonder at his knowledge of sexual intercourse, and the several means of enjoyment used by him; learning from him the sixty-four kinds of pleasure mentioned by Babhravya; continually practising the ways of enjoyment as taught by him, and according to his liking; keeping his secrets; telling him her own desires and secrets; concealing her anger; never neglecting him on the bed when he turns his face towards her; touching any parts of his body according to his wish; kissing and embracing him when he is asleep; showing neither complete shamelessness, nor excessive bashfulness when he meets her, or sees her standing on the terrace of her house from the public road; hating his enemies; loving those who are dear to him; showing a liking for that which he likes; being in high or low spirits according to the state that he is in himself; expressing a curiosity to see his wives; not continuing her anger for a long time; keeping her love for him unexpressed by words, but showing it by deeds, and signs, and hints; giving witty replies to him if he be sufficiently attached to her; abstaining from censuring those who possess the same faults as her own man; wearing anything that may have been given to her by him; wishing to accompany him if he happens to leave the country himself or if he be banished from it by the king; putting on ornaments every day; abstaining from going to public assemblies without him, and accompanying him when he desires her to do so; adapting her tastes, disposition and actions to his liking; and lastly assuring the man of her constancy and love by means of her agents, and receiving money herself, but abstaining from any dispute with her mother with regard to pecuniary matters.

Such is the manner of a courtesan living with a man like a wife, and set forth here for the sake of guidance from the rules of Dattaka. What is not laid down here should be practised according to the custom of the people, and the nature of each individual man.

There are also two verses on the subject as follows:

'The extent of the love of women is not known, even to those who are the objects of their affection, on account of its subtlety, and on account of the avarice, and natural intelligence of womankind.'

'Women are hardly ever known in their true light, though they may love men, or become indifferent towards them, may give them delight, or abandon them, or may extract from them all the wealth that they may possess.'

THERE ARE ALSO SOME VERSES IN CONCLUSION:

'Thus have I written in a few words the "Science of love", after reading the texts of ancient authors, and following the ways of enjoyment mentioned in them.'

'He who is acquainted with the true principles of this science pays regard to Dharma, Artha, Kama, *and to his own experiences, as well as to the teachings of others, and does not act simply on the dictates of his own desire. As for the errors in the science of love which I have mentioned in this work, on my own authority as an author, I have, immediately after mentioning them, carefully censured and prohibited them.'*

'An act is never looked upon with indulgence for the simple reason that it is authorized by the science, because it ought to be remembered that it is the intention of the science, that the rules which it contains should only be acted upon in particular cases. After reading and considering the works of Babhravya and other ancient authors, and thinking over the meaning of the rules given by them, the Kama Sutra *was composed, according to the precepts of Holy Writ, for the benefit of the world, by Vatsyayana, while leading the life of a religious student, and wholly engaged in the contemplation of the Deity.'*

'This work is not intended to be used merely as an instrument for satisfying our desires. A person, acquainted with the true principles of this science, and who preserves his Dharma, Artha, *and* Kama, *and has regard for the practices of the people, is sure to obtain the mastery over his senses.'*

'In short, an intelligent and prudent person, attending to Dharma *and* Artha, *and attending to* Kama *also, without becoming the slave of his passions, obtains success in everything that he may undertake.'*

PICTURE CREDITS

Half title: detail from 'Lovers on a terrace', Pahari, Indian School, 19th century, Bridgeman Images; **Facing title:** 'Lovers on a terrace by a moonlit lake' from the Small Clive Album, Mughal School, 18th century, Bridgeman Images; **Title:** detail from image on page 68; **Imprint:** as image on page 106; **6:** A Prince involved in united intercourse, described by Vatsyayana in his *Kama Sutra*, Bundi, Rajasthan, Rajput School, *c.*1800, Private Collection, Bridgeman Images; **8:** detail from image on page 92; **11:** detail from image on page 43; **12:** 'The private pleasure of Prince Muhammad Agar, son of Aurangzeb' by Rashid, Bikaner, Rajasthan, Rajput School, *c.*1678–98, Bridgeman Images; **13:** detail from image on page 28; **14:** 'Lovers at daybreak', illustration of the musical mode 'Raga Vibhasa', Northern Deccan or Southern Rajasthan, *c.*1675, Bridgeman Images; **20:** 'Young princess playing a tambura', Corbis; **24:** 'Lady on terrace by a lake with four female attendants', miniature painting, 18th century, Corbis; **28:** Erotic scene, Indian School, (18th century), Private Collection, Archives Charmet, Bridgeman Images; **34:** Indian album painting, late 18th–19th century, Corbis; **36:** 'A prince and a lady make love while shooting deer; a buck and a doe come to a stream to drink', Bundi-Kotah, Rajasthan, Rajput School, 1790, Bridgeman Images; **38:** 'The private pleasure of Prince Mohammad Shuja, son of Shah Jahan' by Hunhar, Bikaner, Rajasthan, Rajput School, *c.*1678–98, Bridgeman Images; **39:** detail from 58; **40:** 'A prince and a lady in a combination of two canonical erotic positions listed in the *Kama Sutra*', Bundi, Rajput School, 1790, Bridgeman Images; **43:** 'A royal couple make love in a howdah on the back of an elephant, guided by a servant', Rajasthan, 1790, Bridgeman Images; **45:** detail of Indian couple from 'A Love Scene' by Indian Kishangarh, Rajput School, Corbis; **46:** Erotic scene, Indian School, (18th century), Private Collection, Archives Charmet, Bridgeman Images; **50:** 'Lovers embracing in a forest', Bundi, *c.*1650, Indian School, Bridgeman Images; **54:** 'The private pleasure of Saif Khan' by Chitraman, Bikaner, Rajasthan, Rajput School, *c.*1678–98, Bridgeman Images; **58:** 'The couple making love show the proper posture for female type: Shinkhini; male type: Vrishna' by Anup Chhattar, Bikaner, Rajasthan, Rajput School, *c.*1678–98, Bridgeman Images; **62:** A prince and a lady making love, Werner Forman Archive, Bridgeman Images; **68:** 'The couple making love show the proper posture for female type: Hastini; male type: Ashva' by Govardhan, Bikaner, Rajasthan, Rajput School, *c.*1678–98, Bridgeman Images; **76:** 'The posture of the crow' from the *Kama Sutra*, ecstatic oral intercourse between a prince and a lady among cushions on a carpet, Bundi, Rajasthan, 1790, Rajput School, Bridgeman Images; **86:** 'A lady on a swing, Kangra, Punjab hills', *c.*1790, Mughal School, Bridgeman Images; **92:** 'Malari Ragini', from a Ragamala series, Murshidabad, *c.*1770–75, Mughal School, Bridgeman Images; **96:** 'Couple on a terrace in a garden', Indian School, 18th century, Bridgeman Images; **103:** 'Lovers on a terrace', *c.*1780–1800, Indian School, Bridgeman Images; **106:** 'Lovers on a terrace', Garhwal, *c.*1780–1800, Indian School, Bridgeman Images; **110:** 'Royal lovers on the terrace at night in the moving forward position', from the *Kama Sutra*, Bundi, Rajasthan, Rajput School, late 18th century, Bridgeman Images; **111:** detail from image on page 20; **112:** 'Woman holding a blossom at night', from the Small Clive Album, miniature painting, Mughal School, Corbis; **121:** 'Ramakali Ragini', Ragamala painting, Rajasthan, Indian School, 18th century, Bridgeman Images; **122:** 'Girls bathing, Pahari style', Kangra School, Himachel Pradesh, 18th century, Indian School, Bridgeman Images; **123:** detail from image on page 136; **125:** The private pleasure of Prince Jahandar, son of Jahangir, by Abdul Hamid, Bikaner, Rajasthan, Rajput School, *c.*1678-98, Fitzwilliam Museum, University of Cambridge, UK, Bridgeman Images; **131:** Indian album painting, late 18th–19th century, Corbis; **133:** 'A lady brought in from a night storm', Ragamala miniature painting of a woman going out to meet her lover at night, part of the Madhu Madhavi, Mughal School, Corbis; **136:** 'A couple on horseback beside a moonlit lake', Mark Briscoe, English, 20th century, Bridgeman Images; **144–5:** Album painting, Werner Forman Archive, Bridgeman Images; **146:** 'Women celebrating in a pavilion', possibly a representation of a Mughal court harem, 17th century, Corbis; **150:** 'A couple make love during which the man shoots lions from their pavilion', Rajasthan, Rajput School, 18th century, Bridgeman Images; **151:** detail from image on page 152; **152:** 'Bull among the cows' from the *Kama Sutra*; a prince enjoying five women, Kotah, Rajasthan, Rajput School, 1800, Bridgeman Images; **155:** 'A couple making love whilst riding a camel', Bundi-Kotah, Rajasthan, Rajput style, 1790, Bridgeman Images; **156:** *Kama Sutra* by Vatsyayana: Indian miniature painting, Udaipur, late 18th century, photo © Granger, Bridgeman Images.

The publishers have endeavoured to provide picture credits wherever possible. Any errors or omissions will be corrected in future editions.

160